STUDENT SUCCESS

Stand Up and Be Heard

Taking the Fear Out of Public Speaking at University

Rob Grieve

SAGE

Los Angeles | London | New Delhi
Singapore | Washington DC | Melbourne

SAGE

Los Angeles | London | New Delhi
Singapore | Washington DC | Melbourne

SAGE Publications Ltd
1 Oliver's Yard
55 City Road
London EC1Y 1SP

SAGE Publications Inc.
2455 Teller Road
Thousand Oaks, California 91320

SAGE Publications India Pvt Ltd
B 1/I 1 Mohan Cooperative Industrial Area
Mathura Road
New Delhi 110 044

SAGE Publications Asia-Pacific Pte Ltd
3 Church Street
#10-04 Samsung Hub
Singapore 049483

Editor: Michael Ainsley
Editorial assistant: Amber Turner-Flanders
Production editor: Imogen Roome
Copyeditor: Aud Scriven
Proofreader: Neil Dowden
Indexer: Adam Pozner
Marketing manager: Catherine Slinn
Cover design: Lisa Harper-Wells
Typeset by: C&M Digitals (P) Ltd, Chennai, India
Printed in the UK

First published 2020

Library of Congress Control Number: 2019943693

British Library Cataloguing in Publication data

A catalogue record for this book is available from the British Library

ISBN 978-1-5264-6360-9
ISBN 978-1-5264-6361-6 (pbk)

Contents

About the Author

Dr Rob Grieve is a senior lecturer in Physiotherapy at the University of the West of England and Senior Fellow of the Higher Education Academy (HEA). As a person with a mild stammer, he has found that his many years of teaching have been hugely beneficial in the successful self-management of his speech dysfluency and public speaking fear. The authenticity approach advocated in this book is central to his learning and teaching practice. He has presented nationally at learning and teaching conferences and at other universities on this approach to supporting students with a fear of public speaking. Apart from physiotherapy teaching and research, he is actively involved in running workshops and support for students who have a fear of public speaking. In 2017, he was presented with the Vice Chancellor's Staff Excellence Student Enabling award for his student 'Stand Up and Be Heard' Workshops.

Introduction

Key features of this book include:

- student voices, evaluations and research data from students like you with a fear of public speaking
- lots of practical strategies to reduce your fear of public speaking
- individual activities
- reflective spaces to put down your progress and thoughts
- checklists, summaries
- further resources.

A fear of public speaking is very common in the general population, with a high percentage of people anxious and fearful of standing up and speaking in public. This fear of public speaking can affect social public speaking tasks such as speaking to groups of people or more formal presentations. This anxiety and nervousness about public speaking is particularly common amongst university students, many of whom not only have a fear of public speaking, but also this fear negatively affects their university experience.

Given that many aspects of the student experience include assessments, presentations and public speaking in general (asking questions in a lecture/seminar, talking in groups), this can have serious repercussions for your success and enjoyment as a university student. Public speaking fear may hamper students in their academic achievement, overall university experience and future employment. In essence, public speaking is a life skill and not just confined to university assessments and presentations. Research has shown that a high percentage of students who report a fear of public speaking, would have liked their undergraduate programme to include classes to improve public speaking. However, if as a non-student you have stumbled across this book, the approach and strategies will equally apply to you!

I am an experienced senior lecturer in Physiotherapy, and have many years of experience in preparing and assessing public speaking tasks, including assessed presentations. In assessing many students, I have noticed the fear and difficulty many experience with regard to public speaking and the lack of support provided. As a person who has stammered/stuttered since childhood, I have found that my teaching/public speaking experiences have been hugely beneficial in the successful self-management of my speech dysfluency and anxiety in public speaking. It is from the above academic and personal experience that I have been motivated to support and develop student public speaking skills.

The approach to help those who stammer gain confidence in public speaking is similar for people who are fluent, and is the one I used to develop my Stand Up and Be Heard (SUBH) workshops for university students. The initial ideas for much of the content that led to the development of these workshops and this book are based on a paper published as part of the International Stuttering Awareness Day Online Conference (ISAD 12) (Grieve, 2012) representing countries and individuals from around the world.

This book is based on the tried and tested content and strategies from the workshops to be an *authentic public speaker*, and informed by student evaluations, case studies and a recently conducted qualitative study of student fear of public speaking. The SUBH workshops are extremely popular amongst students and recognised as effective by many staff. Students (and the lecturers marking their presentations) tell me that they work – that they make public speaking a less daunting and more enjoyable task. These workshops also won the Vice Chancellor's Staff Excellence award in July 2017 for student enabling.

Below is a brief overview of the SUBH workshops and their main content.

- Three-hour workshops for students with a fear of public speaking.
- Most workshops have 10–15 students maximum and have been mainly run in the university library.
- Students are involved in group work and sharing ideas throughout in response to the three main areas covered, namely:
  - identification and discussion of issues/fears associated with presenting/public speaking;
  - a review of the authentic approach and strategies to manage the fear of presenting/public speaking;
  - a review of the overall benefits of public speaking, a transferable life skill.
- At the end of the workshop all students complete an evaluation form that ensures the workshops are meeting student needs and updated accordingly.

As you work through this study guide, you will see that the main content covered in the SUBH workshops will be addressed to you as a student with a fear of public speaking. Most of the material I have adapted and developed, and where appropriate references will be supplied from other sources.

We will begin by discussing what exactly a student fear of public speaking is and will then cover how common it is and the specific fears students have. This is important as it sets the scene and enables you to identify which aspects of public speaking you find difficult; it also enables you to focus on the areas you wish to address. One of the key chapters early on will outline the main approach used in the SUBH workshops and the focus in this study guide that will enable you to become an authentic public speaker. The four components that I feel make up an authentic public speaker – namely being present in the moment, being yourself, vulnerability and letting go of perfection – will also be addressed.

It is one thing discussing and advising you to be an authentic public speaker and another to make you more effective and ultimately reduce your fear. Importantly, we will include two chapters on the tried and tested strategies that draw on my own experience, and the wider literature on public speaking, and focus on a hands-on authentic approach. A lot of the emphasis in public speaking is on style over substance and perfection, which increases our fear of public speaking and ultimately does not enable us to meet the needs of our audience.

We will also concentrate on the basics that we as public speakers often forget or do not pay enough attention to. It is often the basics of public speaking preparation that trip up the most confident of public speakers. I have seen many a confident student panic and lose their enjoyment and satisfaction gained from public speaking by not covering the basics before a presentation.

The final third of this study guide will focus on the often neglected aspects of nonverbal behaviour and techniques that can increase your fear and make or break your public speaking efforts. The audience will make assumptions about you even before you open your mouth to speak. Many of those assumptions will be incorrect but will be made by your nonverbal behaviour. Importantly, I have noticed students getting bogged down on issues to do with movement and gestures in public speaking, and so we will address these too to make you more comfortable when standing up and being heard.

Many students state that they fear public speaking and are no good at it. The question to ask here is: how much do you practise your public speaking? You cannot become an effective swimmer or guitar player without practising, and the same goes for public speaking. Regardless of what you may read, no one is born a good public speaker! Some of us take to it more easily, are less fearful of standing up in front of an audience than others, but we still need to work at becoming effective speakers. We will review various ways on how to practise effectively for public speaking and the importance this will have on managing your fear. The strategies to become an authentic public speaker are closely related to your attitude, but are also bound up with the effort and work you put into it.

The final chapter will conclude with the benefits of public speaking and how it can enrich your student and life experience. Many students see no benefit in standing up and being heard as they are often consumed by fear and apprehension. Hopefully by reviewing the benefits of public speaking this will further encourage you to try some of the strategies and ideas put forward in this study guide, whatever your level of study. A fear of public speaking does not only affect first-year undergraduate students; there have been many postgraduate and PhD students on our SUBH workshops who were similarly fearful of speaking in public. More recently I was quite surprised to discover that a few of my teaching colleagues, however experienced, also have a fear of public speaking. You are not alone.

Please do not just take my word for it regarding the usefulness of the material presented in this book – the feedback from the workshop evaluations has been very positive in respect of the application, strategies and benefit to students. Below are a few verbatim comments:

> *'Amazing workshop. The first time I've felt hopeful about public speaking after trying many techniques.'*
>
> *'Really beneficial workshop that I would recommend to anyone with a fear of public speaking.'*
>
> *'This was really useful and should be more encouraged to other students.'*

I do apologise for blowing my own trumpet so to speak, but these comments may boost your confidence that what you have invested in both financially and timewise will be worth your while! This book is unique in that its focus is on authentic public speaking and not perfection, and it is supported by both academic research and my own experience of running fear of public speaking workshops. The move away from perfection and focusing on strategies to become an authentic public speaker is the key to reducing associated public speaking fear and anxiety.

So let's begin.

1

Fear of Public Speaking

OVERVIEW

This chapter will set the scene, lay the groundwork for this study guide and is closely related to the material we cover in the SUBH workshops. The emphasis will be on providing a background to what is public speaking fear, how common it is in students, and what are the main fears that students have associated with various university/college public speaking tasks. The more you are aware of your public speaking fears and that you are not alone, the easier it is to manage those fears. The fears we discuss are based on feedback from students on the workshops, a recently completed research study and wider evidence. You will also have the chance to complete some *individual activities* personal to you that may help in your understanding of your fear of public speaking.

What is public speaking fear?

A fear of public speaking can be mild to debilitating and may have a negative effect on students' experience and future employment. Varying terms are used to describe a fear of public speaking and are often used interchangeably, such as 'stage fright', 'communication apprehension', 'public speaking anxiety' and 'glossophobia'. The term 'glossophobia' comes from the Greek *glōssa*, meaning tongue, and *phobos*, fear or dread, and is related to a fear of public speaking. Many students have a fear of public speaking, regardless of the various terms we can apply.

A fear of public speaking can exist in isolation with no anxieties about personal relationships or other social situations. Importantly, you may only have a fear of public speaking with no associated mental health issues, given this fear is very normal and common amongst the general population. Apart from the more obvious fear and anxiety associated with presentations, a large percentage of the student experience revolves around a range of generic public speaking skills from asking questions in a lecture/seminar, talking in groups, oral assessments and presentations. Undergraduate students will be tackling tasks demanding intellectual achievement as well as public speaking skills (Ferreira Marinho et al., 2017). The range of generic public speaking skills will be more fully addressed at the end of this chapter, and lead onto the main approach and strategies for tackling your fear of public speaking.

How common is the fear of public speaking?

The well-known US comedian Jerry Seinfeld once famously commented along the lines that people's number one fear is public speaking, feared more than death, and if you go to a funeral, you're better off in the casket than doing the eulogy. Although amusing and often quoted, this statement is not entirely true!

Some of the longstanding views held on how common public speaking fear is relate back to an article based on a survey published in the London *Sunday Times* in 1973, entitled 'What People Usually Fear'. According to Dwyer and Davidson (2012), the findings in this survey have been quoted in many public speaking textbooks, leading to the common belief that people fear giving a speech more than death.

In a research paper entitled 'Is Public Speaking Really More Feared than Death?', Dwyer and Davidson (2012) found that the original 1973 survey asked respondents to pick items from a list representing 14 fearful situations. Some of the fearful situations included speaking before a group, heights, financial problems and escalators. Importantly, the survey did not ask participants to rank the 14 fears or select their top fear; however, they reported that *speaking before a group* was the most selected common fear, but it was not selected as the top fear *because that question was never asked*. Interestingly, a recent survey by Chapman University (2018) of average Americans' fears found that public speaking has now dropped to number 59 on the complete list of fears. This fear of public speaking amongst the general population appears to be less than in previous years, although if you look at lists of phobias public speaking (glossophobia) is recognised as a common fear.

In respect of student fears of public speaking, *public speaking is a common fear* was selected by 61% of US college students;

however, the top three fears were death, followed by speaking before a group and financial problems (Dwyer and Davidson, 2012). A survey on the impact of social anxiety on student learning and wellbeing from two universities in the UK found that 80% of students surveyed reported that public speaking/presentations were associated with frequent social anxiety (Russell and Topham, 2012). More recently a study of undergraduate students in the USA found that 64% reported a fear of public speaking (Ferreira Marinho et al., 2017). As you can see the evidence from the USA and UK points clearly to the fact that students have a fear of public speaking.

Recently, we conducted a qualitative survey of fears of public speaking with students attending our SUBH workshops (Grieve et al., 2019). One of the four open questions asked the following: 'Does your fear of public speaking affect your student experience of higher education?' Related to this open question, one of the six themes that emerged from the research was that a fear of public speaking had a *'Negative effect on university experience'* for most of the students who had attended the SUBH workshops. Below are some of the student voices (comments/quotes) in relation to a fear of public speaking and university experience.

Student Voices

Fear of public speaking and university experience

'I feel I would be able to attain better marks if I were able to present more effectively.'

'Yes, as the anxiety is at times uncontrollable.'

'It sometimes stops me from participating in discussions.'

'It has put me off doing modules in the past because of a presentation element.'

'Yes, not really asking questions so can understand things.'

'This scares me, as I am only just learning my postgraduate subject of environmental law.'

'Yes, it can do as sometimes my fear obstructs what my educational focus is meant to be.'

'Yes, it takes the fun out of speaking at presentations.'

'Brings anxiety to speak in class.'

'I actively never attempted a degree until now (age 40) in part because I knew I would be expected to present and did not feel able.'

As stated previously, and shown by the evidence above and student voices, you are not alone, and this is a comforting fact and an important factor in addressing your fear of public speaking.

Specific student fears of public speaking

Before we identify specific student fears related to public speaking, a useful starting point in dealing with your fear of public speaking is to first identify what your main issues/fears are of standing up and talking to a group of people. When you are aware of which aspects may cause your fear, you will be in a better position to make some changes and address those fears.

Individual Activity

You are not alone! In the space below jot down what would be your main issues/fears when standing up and talking to a group of people.

AUTHOR'S EXPERIENCE

As a university lecturer and someone with a stammer (that has improved dramatically since I stood up and was heard), I used to spend all my time worrying about my style (how I would come across) over substance (instead of the content). Many years ago, at an exam board I stumbled over introducing myself (very common with people who stammer) in front of about 40 academics and one of my colleagues chuckled at my misfortune. When speaking to him about it later he thought I had choked (briefly) on a biscuit! Related to my fear of getting the words out smoothly and focusing too much on style over substance, I used to tap my foot before a stammer-inducing word to smooth its passage into the presentation. After presenting on a one-day workshop, one of the evaluations commented on the over-enthusiastic and persistent foot tapping by the presenter during the day!

Student Voices

Fear of public speaking

Example 1

'I have had a fear of public speaking for as long as I can remember and avoided it wherever possible. When presentations were compulsory during school or sixth form I would feel incredibly anxious throughout the preceding days and moments before the event I would be shaky and breathless. These symptoms only worsened during the presentation and I would rush my way through to the end.

One particularly negative experience of public speaking remains clear in my mind: I had to present in a group for my Gold Duke of Edinburgh Award to over 70 individuals, which was a much larger audience than usual. During this presentation I felt incredibly anxious and had to stop numerous times during my very short talk to unsuccessfully catch my breath. I was shaking, sweating and stumbling, and I burst into tears once it ended due to embarrassment. This experience unfortunately heightened my fear; however, I mostly managed to avoid public speaking until two compulsory presentation exams during my final year of university. During the second presentation assessment, I felt my symptoms return as usual; my mouth was dry and I was incredibly breathless. However, I believe I had been unnerved by a breakdown I experienced the night before due to the stress of such a long period of revision and exams.'

Example 2

'For me, a main fear of speaking in front of a group of people was the thought of these people thinking negatively about me based on my presentation. My response to this anxiety often meant that I would avoid speaking in front of large groups and often not even speak up in seminars as my heart rate became so high.'

Example 3

'I spent years believing that I must be the only person to have an 'irrational' fear of speaking publicly and I felt embarrassed at how much my anxiety would take over during presentations. Five years after my first degree and I am faced with the same inevitable dread that university presentations entail, and it turns out it's not just me that feels this way. What I feared the most about public speaking was mainly judgement from peers and making no sense.'

Regardless of the terminology or definitions used a fear of public speaking can affect you in many ways. It can affect the speaker physically with a dry mouth, increased blood pressure, blushing, sweating, irregular breathing, and emotionally in the form of feelings of humiliation and concerns about looking foolish (Kushner, 2004).

We will first address some of the specific physical signs and symptoms, and then cover the emotional aspects of public speaking in the next section on internal and external fears.

Physical signs and symptoms

Most of the physical symptoms are due to the 'fight or flight' response, a physiological reaction that occurs in response to a stressful situation, for example being attacked by a dog or, less serious, standing up to speak. Due to this acute stress, the body reacts physically, and the immediate response is the activation of the autonomic and sympathetic nervous system due to the sudden release of hormones. The 'flight or fight' response was first described by American physiologist Walter Bradford Cannon as early as 1915, who studied the effects of intense emotional states on the body, which led him to the experimental identification of adrenaline and noradrenaline and the fight/flight reflex (Taylor, 2000).

The 'fight or flight' response has been well described in the literature, and the main physical effects on the body, in relation to a fearful or stressful situation, are due to the sudden increased levels of cortisol, adrenaline and other hormones. These physical changes are there to enable you to respond to an eminent danger or stressor. The major physiological changes are as follows (Martin, 2003):

- Heart rate increases.
- Blood pressure increases.
- Blood vessels constrict.
- Blood sugar levels increase.
- Blood flow is directed to major organs.
- Breathing is deeper and faster.
- Perspiration increases.
- Digestion stops.

All of the above physiological changes can result in the noticeable pale or flushed skin and visible trembling and shaking that may occur when you are about to start public speaking. The 'fight or flight' response is a normal reaction to something that you may find stressful and is usually short lived, resolving once the threat or danger is no longer present.

Internal and external fears

Another way to try and understand public speaking fears is to divide them into internal and external fears. Internal fears are how we view the speaking situation, in relation to the delivery and the feelings the speaker is experiencing, whereas external fears are largely related to the audience during the speech. Dividing public speaking fears in this way will help you to further understand and identify your specific fears of public speaking. A speaker's anxiety related to forgetting information and freezing up during the speech represents an internal fear, while anxiety about being the focal point of attention from the audience constitutes an external fear (LeFebvre et al., 2018).

Now that you have identified your main fears associated with public speaking in the individual activity above, let's see if any of these are similar to those fears identified below by other university/college students. In a recent study in 2018 on self-described fears related to public speaking of 828 university/college students in the USA (Le Febvre et al., 2018: 352–7), the researchers identified 12 common categories or themes from students on an introductory communication course that included both internal and external fears.

Overall, the most commonly reported fear by students (30%) was the external fear *audience responses*, which was related to perceived attitudes from the audience towards the speaker. This category included judgement from the audience and being the focus of attention, conspicuousness (being the focus of attention, which students found challenging) and non-interaction. The next most commonly reported fear (23%) was *inability to self-regulate*, and the researchers described this as students' fear about their own performance during a speech, which included fears about their own recall of information or their inability to remember the presentation content during a speech. Interestingly, the other nine categories were much less reported, with the third most common fear, *dysfluency*, only reported by 8% of students, and included fears about not speaking fluently and using too many verbal fillers (e.g. um, ah, erm, like, huh) (Le Febvre et al., 2018).

Further to the qualitative survey of public speaking fears of students attending our SUBH workshops (Grieve et al., 2019), one of the open questions asked was: 'What are your main issues/fears in public speaking (including presentations)?' The three main themes related to the most common responses from students who had a fear of public speaking were *fear of being judged* (external fear related to the audience), *uncertainty about the topic* (internal fear) and *physical symptoms* (a combination of internal and external fears and a clear example of the physical signs/symptoms and 'flight or fight' response to an external stimulus/fear). As you can see, these main fears are similar to those in the previous study (Le Febvre et al., 2018) described above, and are a mix of internal and external fears.

Below are some of the student voices (comments/quotes) in relation to the three main issues/fears in public speaking identified above. Once you have read these student voices on their main issues/fears, I would strongly encourage you to complete the individual activity below. In completing this you will soon realise that you and your fellow students share many of the same public speaking fears, and this in turn will increase your insight and motivation to change.

Student Voices

Examples of fear of being judged

'I think I have a deeply rooted fear around being seen and heard.'

'Don't like people looking at me.'

'Standing up in front of people.'

'Talking in front of a large audience.'

'Fear of standing up in front of a group of people who are focusing on me.'

'Worried of what people will think.'

'Fear of being judged. (This comment was expressed by many students in the study.)'

'Worry that people are not interested.'

'The audience may not be interested in what I say.'

'That people will laugh at me.'

Examples of uncertainty about the topic

'Making a mistake.'

'Forgetting parts of what I need to say.'

'Forgetting what I'm supposed to say, causing me to mess up even more.'

'Coming across that I don't know what I'm on about.'

'My main issue/fear in public speaking is that I am afraid of any kind of mistake.'

'Getting it wrong.'

Physical symptoms

'Physical clues I am nervous, e.g. shaking hands, tongue tied speech.'

'Panic attack that would stop me communicating.'

'Going red/blushing.'

'Throat seems dry, hands sweaty and emotional experience is overwhelming enough to cause me to become tearful.'

'Going red when I start to talk.'

'Physical symptoms of stress.'

Further to verbally expressing your fears of public speaking, why not try to express these visually. Sometimes this may be more effective, especially if an emotion or experience is difficult to explain in words. Drawing, painting or using specific colours may be a nonverbal visual way to communicate your fears, especially if English is not your first language. We have many international students on our SUBH workshops who would also benefit from using a drawing, painting or any other art form to express their feelings. You do not have to be a talented artist or actively involved in the arts to benefit from this approach to representing what you fear in public speaking. Drawing has been found to be effective for students to share and identify their fears in public speaking (Rattine-Flaherty, 2014).

Individual Activity

You are definitely not alone!

You may also be able to relate to the above themes and comments from fellow university students with a fear of public speaking. With a pen or pencil circle or tick the themes/comments you can relate to. As shown above, the more you are aware of your fears and can acknowledge that other students may feel the same, the greater your understanding, and this will help you in tackling your fear of public speaking.

In concluding this section on specific fears of public speaking, it is important to note that some students may have broader mental health issues that may have a direct impact on public speaking and social interaction, namely social anxiety disorder (SAD).

SAD is a mental health diagnosis and is classified in the *Diagnostic and Statistical Manual of Mental Disorders* (DSM 5) (American Psychiatric Association, 2013). According to the DSM 5, some of the main characteristics in their SAD definition are: a persistent fear of one or more social or performance situations in which the person is exposed to unfamiliar people or to possible scrutiny by others; exposure to the feared situation invokes anxiety which may take the form of a panic attack; the feared situations are avoided or endured with intense anxiety and distress, and this may interfere significantly with the person's normal routine, occupation, social activities or relationships: this fear, anxiety or avoidance is persistent, lasting six or more months, and is not due to the direct physiological effects of substances (drugs, medications) or a general medical condition.

In the SUBH workshops I briefly mention and discuss SAD and how this may be the reason for some students' fear of public speaking. I therefore also recommend that they may need further intensive psychological therapy (cognitive behavioural therapy (CBT), counselling, etc.) and academic support that are beyond the scope of the SUBH workshops and my expertise. In the same light, although this book may be helpful, I would advise that you may need to seek further psychological and professional counselling if you have SAD or any other mental health issue that interferes with your daily living and impacts on your public speaking, and is therefore beyond the scope of this study guide.

Student fear of public speaking – not just presentations

This chapter and study guide mainly focus on public speaking fear in relation to presentations. Presentations appear to be the aspect of public speaking that most students find most challenging; however, other public speaking activities can also present challenges and fears. Apart from presentations this section will briefly review seminars, lectures, practical exams/viva voce and extra-curricular activities. In Chapter 8, we will further review the range of public speaking activities you may encounter at university and their associated benefits.

Presentations – As a student many of the modules that will make up your programme of study will be assessed by a presentation. Most module leaders will give you clear guidelines for what your presentation should cover. Many students find presentations very daunting and fear provoking, not to mention the additional pressure of having a presentation graded with implications for an overall degree classification. Apart from giving presentations at university, you may be involved in conferences as a postgraduate student discussing your research or other related university projects. Although various public speaking skills are necessary, most student fears about public speaking relate to presentations and the act of standing up in front of a group of classmates, lecturers or external examiners.

Seminars – Due to large cohort sizes, many programmes of study use seminars as an opportunity for students to learn in smaller groups. In seminars students are often asked to read a paper beforehand and then discuss the findings with other students. Public speaking skills are required here as you may be asked to discuss concepts and ideas amongst a few of you or across the seminar group. Asking questions and debating issues are aspects of public speaking required in seminar groups.

Lectures – Public speaking skills are needed in asking a question, particularly in a lecture hall with a 100 or so students. When I give a lecture to many students, the number who ask questions is normally quite low. This is understandable as described above, as the student may feel uncomfortable being the centre of attention or being judged by peers if they ask a 'silly' question. Many academics have issues with lecture settings as the opportunity for two-way communication and interactive learning is reduced. I ask students to split into small groups in a lecture hall to discuss issues, which is less scary than standing up in front of a 100 or more of one's peers. However, there will be times when you may need to ask questions related to aspects of a lecture you are unsure about.

Practical exams and viva voce – Depending on the programme of study you are on, you may need to attend practical exams or vivas. For the viva exam you will often be asked questions by a number of examiners, either seated or standing up. In many healthcare and other programmes, there are practical exams where you may need to show assessment or treatment skills. For both types of assessment your public speaking skills are essential to communicate ideas and discuss concepts.

Extra-curricular activities – Apart from the formal teaching and learning input many students will be involved in extra-curricular activities, such as student union activities, clubs and society membership. Student representative roles, setting up or involvement in a student society may all require public speaking in one form or another. I have been involved in running workshops for student reps, those on leadership courses or those students acting as peer assisted learners. Some universities have student ambassadors, who often have to speak to groups of students on open days while taking guided tours of a university campus and also present to an auditorium full of parents and potential students.

Individual Activity

What other public speaking opportunities are you involved in that are included above?

List those public speaking activities that you find challenging and the reason(s) for this.

Chapter summary

This chapter has set the scene for this study guide by laying the foundations in respect of what is public speaking fear and how common it is in university students. The section on specific student fears was supported by the evidence, which I feel adds to the credibility of the material, and expressed in terms of student voices which you should have been able to relate to. The chapter concluded with a brief section on the various university public speaking skills and activities required apart from just presentations. Throughout this chapter there were several individual activities that I hope you will complete to ensure the material covered has meaning and is relevant to you. Finally, please do not forget to complete the reflective space below as doing so will be beneficial in your public speaking journey.

Reflective Space

Using this reflective space will give you an opportunity to review and consolidate what has been covered in this chapter. This might be something that you have not done much of, but in my experience, and those of students in the SUBH workshops, it has proved really helpful.

What could you take home from this chapter in respect of understanding public speaking fear and how it may affect you?

2

Authenticity, Not Perfection

OVERVIEW

This chapter will discuss the key take home message: to be an authentic public speaker. Once you recognise this and move away from unrealistic perfection, all else falls into place. The focus on authenticity is a move away from many 'perfection'-based presentation skill texts and approaches. This chapter will discuss and explore what it means to be an authentic public speaker. The rest of the book will then focus on specific strategies to become an authentic public speaker, and in turn help you to reduce your fear of public speaking.

What do we mean by being authentic?

The word 'authentic' is commonly used in everyday life, from describing a piece of antique jewellery or a piece of artwork to the authenticity of an online bank transaction. Dictionary definitions of authenticity describe something as authentic if it is real, true or what people say it is, or being genuine. Historically, many disciplines within the arts and sciences have long sought to define who one 'really' is, with contemporary psychological views of authenticity owing a debt to the works of philosophy (Kernis and Goldman, 2006).

We will not be delving into any deep psychological or philosophical theories but will focus on the main approach of this study guide, i.e. being an authentic public speaker. However, according to Mengers, (2014) although interest and theories on authenticity have existed for centuries, only recently has evidence been gathered that shows the link between authenticity and wellbeing and that our level of authenticity relates to our wellbeing. This association between authenticity and wellbeing is valid in this approach, given the fears that students exhibit in public speaking (Chapter 1). On a personal note, as soon as I adopted an authentic approach, a lot of the feelings of dread and anxiety I associated with public speaking were greatly reduced.

Any approach that increases wellbeing is very relevant in the present university climate, as there is a strong recognition of issues regarding student mental health and how this has negatively impacted on the student experience. This is therefore further motivation to become an authentic public speaker, which will in turn hopefully reduce or manage your fear of public speaking. It is important to note, however, that having a bit of fear and nervousness is not an entirely negative thing, and we will discuss this in the later chapters dealing with specific strategies to reach your authentic public speaker goal. Have a go at the individual activity below, which will be a good starting point for your understanding of what makes an authentic public speaker.

Individual Activity

Write down in this box what your understanding is of an authentic public speaker.

An authentic public speaker is:

Further to the above activity, you may have a different idea about what an authentic public speaker is or how they may speak in public. In the SUBH workshop, we focus on the following components that may enable you to become an authentic public speaker:

- Being present in the moment
- Be yourself
- Vulnerability
- Let go of perfectionism

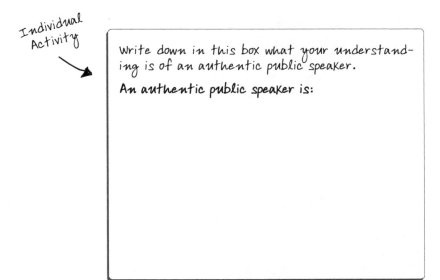

A key point that we stress in the SUBH workshops is that becoming an authentic public speaker does not happen overnight, it takes time and practice to implement. What does change very quickly, as we have found with many students, is the realisation that striving for perfection and style over substance increases the public speaking fear level. Most students, and hopefully you also, like the message and approach related to becoming an authentic public speaker. The simplicity and real world application seem to strike a chord with students.

Four components that make an authentic public speaker

I would encourage you to complete the individual activities related to the four components discussed in this section, to enable you to identify where you are and how you could become an authentic public speaker.

Being present in the moment

The concept of being present in the moment is sometimes used in relation to the term 'mindfulness'. It is not within the scope of this study guide to discuss mindfulness, although I would encourage you to access the many resources and workshops available on mindfulness (see Further Resources). Mindfulness is most commonly defined as the state of being attentive to and aware of what is taking place in the present, an optimal moment-to-moment experience, which may enhance wellbeing (Brown and Ryan, 2003). This being immersed in the moment, specifically focused on our public speaking task, is something those of us with a fear of public speaking may find difficult.

One of the real fears that many people have in public speaking is standing up in front of an audience. In the previous chapter we identified a key theme in our research study, namely *fear of being judged*, which was expressed by many students in relation to public speaking.

In the SUBH workshops, when asking students to list their main fears, these focused on being the centre of attention with every eye in the room trained on them. With a fear of public speaking, the temptation is to concentrate on finishing this presentation or public speaking task as fast as possible and not be present in the moment. The other strategy that we use is to try and think of anything but what we are currently doing, i.e. speaking in public. I remember many years ago just wanting to finish the presentation, focusing on the end instead of the present activity – a strategy that did nothing to reduce my fear of public speaking or improve my wellbeing.

Individual Activity

Try and think how you felt when last speaking in public and your thoughts were everywhere but in that moment.

Did you feel more relaxed and in control?

In being present in the moment, your focus is on the speaking task at hand and being OK with standing in front of an audience. Being present in the moment really means being absorbed in the present speaking task, focused on meeting the needs of the audience and not being preoccupied by your fears and anxieties. Importantly, being present in the moment demands that you concentrate on the audience and what you are about to say. This is easier than it sounds, and though it may take a while to achieve is a strong component of the authentic public speaker.

There are a number methods associated with mindfulness, including, posture, internal visualisation (to be discussed in Chapter 7) and breathing, that are advocated to be present in the moment. In the SUBH workshops I argue that if you wish to be your authentic self, steer away from perfection and meet the audience needs that should ensure you are in the moment. The strategies to be authentic (see Chapter 3 and Chapter 4) should hopefully help you to achieve this element of authentic public speaking. Remember, an audience will quickly recognise if you are fully engaged in your public speaking task, or look as though you do not care or want to get out of there as fast as possible!!

Be yourself

In the words of Oscar Wilde, 'Be yourself; everyone else is already taken'. Recent research suggests that the experience of expressing one's authentic self may reduce aspects of social anxiety disorder, of which a fear of public speaking is an example (Plasencia et al., 2016). An audience will more likely trust you and your message if they feel that you are being genuine and speaking from the heart.

In the early days of my lecturing career, and when presenting on one-day physical therapy workshops to paying clinicians, I used to spend a lot of the time preoccupied with my speech dysfluency. As a person with a mild stammer, I would often block or get stuck on certain words and try different covert strategies to avoid stammering. The focus was on how I was saying words and phrases instead of what was being said. After one physical therapy workshop, a participant remarked on the amount of foot tapping (which helped expel a blocked word) that I had actively engaged in during the day. I was not really being myself and was trying to hide or cover up my stammer. For the first few years of my teaching and doing public speaking, this cover-up was stressful and put a lot of pressure on me as a public speaker.

After about five years, I finally plucked up the courage to use self-disclosure and do some 'verbal housekeeping', not the usual pre-public speaking housekeeping issues related to fire exits and available toilet facilities. Before any lecture or public speaking task, I would do some 'verbal housekeeping' before the audience along the lines of *'Just to inform you all I have a mild stammer that may cause me to block, hesitate or deviate from the odd word ... not that I do not know what I am talking about, just cannot get the words out! This will give you more time to write up your notes.'*

This invariably resulted in a bit of laughter and chuckling, but it got the audience on side and allowed me to be myself. Overnight, I became more authentic and effective as a public speaker. More importantly, I no longer view the public speaking opportunity as something to be feared. I still use self-disclosure the first time I teach a group of students or do any form of public speaking.

Being yourself does not mean that you should not try or strive to be an effective public speaker. In the following chapters we will clearly outline how to be an authentic, effective and less fearful public speaker. Audiences will very quickly tune out if you put on a front and try to be someone else!

Individual Activity

Try and think how you could be more yourself in public speaking.

What have you tried to hide from the audience that you feel is preventing you from being an authentic public speaker?

Vulnerability

One of the real challenges of public speaking, as discussed earlier, is standing up in front of an audience and being the focal point for their attention. Standing alone and putting yourself out there in front of the audience, with nowhere to hide. One thing I have learned is that vulnerability does not equate with weakness or the inability to be an effective public speaker. According to Brown (2015), the perception that vulnerability is weakness is a widely accepted myth and we need to appreciate the courage behind vulnerability – that it is also the source of authenticity. This concept of vulnerability in relation to how we lead our lives, as well as leadership, courage and as a strength, has become more widely accepted and documented. In 2010 Brené Brown delivered a TED Talk called *The Power of Vulnerability* and has since published widely on the topic of vulnerability. In our SUBH workshops I always direct students to her TED Talk and further literature. I would strongly encourage you to follow their lead.

To be authentic as a public speaker is to be vulnerable to an extent. However much we plan, prepare and practise our public speaking task, there is always the possibility that we may have a bad day, the audience may not be as receptive as we would like, the IT system is on the blink or someone has just asked a really challenging question. A year ago, I remember standing at one end of a very long and narrow lecture hall with 100+ students in attendance. The podium (on wheels) and PC were miles away from the front row of students. In my wisdom, I attempted to move the podium closer, only to disconnect the main power cable with the resultant blank screen and immediate panic on my behalf!

As described above, there may be many and varied internal and external reasons for our vulnerability, the main one being the mere fact of being a human with innate strengths and weaknesses. Many students feel vulnerable when attending university or college. A younger student, who has just finished school and is away from home for the first time, may feel 'homesick' and miss family and friends in this new environment. An older/mature student may have left a job to study full-time, with all the associated financial pressures and juggling family responsibilities. During the university programme of study, students may feel unsure about their ability to write essays, perform in exams or give an assessed presentation.

A public speaker who is aware of their vulnerability as a human, and still has the courage to put themself out there, will gain the respect and trust of an audience.

Importantly, you are not helpless or incapable of the task at hand but just aware of your vulnerability. One of the exciting aspects of vulnerability is that it gives us the freedom in public speaking to be ourselves, as too often we are constrained by rules and supposed ways of speaking in public. We are aware of our vulnerability but plan to embrace, acknowledge and not suppress this fundamental part of ourselves.

Individual Activity

Try and think how your vulnerability may positively influence or affect your public speaking.

How would being aware of that vulnerability change your approach to public speaking?

Let go of perfectionism

This fourth component in becoming an authentic public speaker is strongly related to being yourself and the vulnerability that we have discussed above.

Recent newspaper articles in *The New York Times*, 'More College Students Seem to Be Majoring in Perfectionism' (Adams, 2018), and the *Guardian*, '"My Brain Feels Like It's Been Punched": The Intolerable Rise of Perfectionism' (Cocozza, 2018), have highlighted the rise of university student perfection. It appears that students' drive for perfectionism in relation to their studies and fuelled by social media may be affecting their mental health. Both newspaper articles in the USA and UK are based on a recent study by Curran and Hill (2017) that analysed findings from a perfectionism scale completed by 41,641 American, Canadian and British university/college students. The overall findings indicate that young people today perceive that others are more demanding of them, are more demanding of others and are more demanding of themselves.

I see this striving for perfection in students on a regular basis, in relation to written and practice-based module assessments. It is completely understandable that many students aim to achieve as high a grade as possible, as the stakes are also high regarding personal ambitions, financial investment and potential job prospects. The downside is that many students are placing huge demands on themselves which may have some negative consequences for their wellbeing and mental health.

This striving for perfection manifests itself in public speaking, and is often the default position of many students and people who have a fear of attempting public speaking tasks. Students often focus on style, a slickness of presentation over substance, which in turn may increase the pressure on themselves and their public speaking fear. A few mistakes and forgetting the occasional word will normally be forgiven by an audience, if they believe and trust in your overall message. There seems to be an over-emphasis on the perfect delivery, devoid of verbal fillers (umms or aahs) and cutting out all our usual mannerisms. To be authentic we do not need to radically change our way of speaking.

A colleague of mine, who has repeatedly won the lecturer of the year award at a university in Australia, has a severe stammer. He may not be perfect in the traditional sense of speech delivery, but his knowledge and passion for the subject outweigh any fluency issues. It's important to note here also that fluency, a slick presentation, does not equal good communication. A few years ago, I went to on a day-long presentation workshop and was dismayed on the perfection focus in relation to the delivery of a presentation. Delivery is important but is only one aspect of public speaking that often causes a lot of dismay to students and those involved in public speaking. To add insult to injury, I was informed that according to the facilitator I was the 'best public speaker with a stammer' they had encountered.

Student Voice

No one is perfect

'My biggest fear with public speaking was getting muddled with words or having a mind blank due to my dyslexia, but what the SUBH workshop taught me was that no one is perfect!'

Public speaking is not about perfection

'I have always strived for perfection. However, the course made me realise that public speaking isn't perfect and needs to be adaptable due to the audience. It has made me aware that some of my fears are good aspects of public speaking, such as pausing, using prompts as aids and to focus on the message I am aiming to convey to the audience.'

In conclusion, Ni (2013) in *Psychology Today* has two great points in relation to public speaking and perfection:

1. *Don't expect perfection from yourself* – None of us are perfect, yet when it comes to public speaking we kick ourselves over every little perceived mistake we make. This is a very valid point and I am sure it is one you

can relate to – I certainly can. Often in our push for perfection in public speaking we cannot attain our high standards or unrealistic expectations and have then put undue pressure on ourselves.

2. *Self-worth* – Whether you're good at public speaking or not has nothing to do with your value as a person. And with regard to the first point, we often take it very personally when we are not as good at public speaking as we would like to be.

These points on perfection have impacted on me and I am sure many students have struggled with public speaking in the past. I can remember on quite a few occasions when a public speaking task did not go as well as I would have liked it to, with the feelings of self-depreciation lasting for a few days. Since we are putting ourselves on the line by standing up and being heard, we often feel judged and open to scrutiny, and therefore take it personally.

Individual Activity

Can you remember when striving for perfection caused you to fear speaking in public?

Which aspects of public speaking perfection could you drop to decrease the fear factor?

Our SUBH workshop evaluations since 2015 have indicated that the authentic approach, i.e. moving away from perfection, has many positive benefits and helps students manage their fear of public speaking. Many have emailed me and shared their positive public speaking experiences after focusing on becoming an authentic public speaker.

Chapter summary

The material covered in this chapter on becoming an authentic public speaker included four components, namely being present in the moment, be yourself, vulnerability and let go of perfectionism. Being an authentic speaker has resulted in many students changing their whole outlook to public speaking. Hopefully, you will adopt the authentic approach that will enable you to manage your fear and become an effective public speaker. It's important to note here that this authentic approach will not happen overnight, but the more you do it the easier and more automatic it will become. In the next few chapters we will review some simple, tried and tested strategies for becoming an authentic public speaker. Please use the reflective space below to consider where you stand in respect of authenticity presently, and whether you feel this is something you could embrace.

Reflective Space

Using this reflective space will give you an opportunity to review and consolidate what has been covered in this chapter. This might be something that you have not done much of, but in my experience and those of students in the SUBH workshops, it has proven really helpful.

Answer the questions below and reflect on which of these four components in becoming an authentic public speaker you feel you already possess and which of these need to be addressed:

1. Are you present in the moment when speaking in public?
2. Are you yourself when speaking in public?
3. Are you aware of your vulnerability in public speaking? Do you see this as a strength?
4. How do you let go of perfectionism when public speaking?

3

Strategies to Be Authentic – Part One

OVERVIEW

This chapter will build on the take-home message of being an authentic speaker and give you the reader strategies to achieve this goal. The strategies in this chapter and the next have been tried and tested in our SUBH workshops, with most students finding at least two or more of help in reducing their fear of public speaking. As discussed earlier, public speaking refers to any speaking task involving standing up and speaking to people. Most of the emphasis in this chapter is on presentations, but can be related to any public speaking activity including seminars, peer support, and clinical or work placements.

While reading through the strategies, please always have at the forefront of your mind that to really get to grips with these strategies, become a more authentic public speaker and reduce your fear you need to practise and adequately prepare. Due to the importance of effective practice, we will be devoting a whole chapter to this topic further on in the book (Chapter 7).

We will now review the following strategies below that may help you manage your fear and become a more authentic public speaker. In reviewing each of these, we will include practical steps to apply this strategy to your public speaking:

- Know your subject
- Keep it simple
- Know your audience
- Tell stories
- Creativity

Know your subject

'Knowledge is power' (Francis Bacon, 1597)

One of the key issues in relation to a fear of public speaking, and a very simple strategy to understand, is that of knowing your subject. Basically, this means you need to be very familiar with and ensure you have an in-depth knowledge of your topic, which allows you to be yourself and focus on the message and meet the needs of your audience. This in turn will help you manage or reduce your fear. An audience may be initially blinded by a slick presenter, but this will soon wear off when they realise that this is style over substance.

Many students ignore the knowledge foundation of their public speaking task, especially in presentations. If you build a house with limited or shaky foundations, it will eventually fall down. If you give a presentation and you have superficial knowledge of the topic, you will eventually be found out! Student fear may be strongly related to a lack of confidence and comfort in the presentation topic. In our SUBH workshops many students identify a fear of not being able to answer questions related to their presentation. If you have a good knowledge base, this would immediately resolve this common fear/issue with public speaking.

Many presentation texts focus on the importance of delivery and do not spend enough time or place sufficient emphasis on the importance of really knowing the topic. I remember going to a one-day workshop on presentation and public speaking with no focus at all on the knowledge base and information aspect of the presentation. The emphasis was on delivery, use of voice, style over substance. This is not sound advice for public speaking, and even worse advice in a university setting where you may be assessed on your subject knowledge. Do not be tempted to skip spending time on this key strategy, as it will reap public speaking benefits in the long run.

In the university academic environment, when we give an assessed presentation and have limited subject knowledge, our focus on delivery may just disguise our lack of knowledge. Will the audience eventually click that we are more style than substance, will we be found out? How do you think this will affect your confidence and increase your fear factor? We may also try to present ourselves as something we are not, therefore reducing our authenticity to cover up our lack of subject/topic knowledge.

Individual Activity

Think of a time when you gave a presentation and did not have a full grasp of the topic. Did you feel comfortable and confident or did it increase your public speaking fear?

Practical steps to apply this strategy to your public speaking

Next time you make a presentation, adopt the following steps. (Take note that some of these steps are further developed in other chapters and will be signposted.)

- *Read the module presentation guidelines*
    - Read the guidelines (see Chapter 5) fully and make sure you are clear on which topic/subject your presentation is on. Also check on which aspects of the topic you are required to address, and focus on knowing specifically what's being asked of you. Find all of this out if you're not sure. It is important you are clear on the knowledge and understanding you need to demonstrate.
- *Reading material and resources*
    - The knowledge you display of the subject in your presentation is gained from the reading material and relevant resources. It is worthwhile remembering here that while we live in an age where

there is an abundance of material that is available online, some of that material will be of poor quality and unreliable. It is therefore important we are critical and aware of the limitations of some reading material and its origins. Some of our students have cited material from dubious websites and sources that are unreliable and not trustworthy.

- Traditionally, a search strategy would consist of identifying key terms and then using databases from your university library to search for relevant publications. Many university online modules have a reading list of recommended textbooks and journal articles that would be a trustworthy and reliable source of knowledge. Your lecturer may point you in the direction of valid reading material and resources in the lecture notes. Speak to your university library staff and search the library catalogues for relevant material you can trust.

- *Read, read and read some more*
  - It is crucial that you read around the subject, initially just getting a feel for it (breadth), and then in depth, i.e. specifically related to your topic. Try and read from plenty of textbooks or journal articles to really get to know and understand your subject. Once you feel you have read in sufficient breadth and depth for your topic start to write a summary or overview of the key points that could be presented in the timescale allowed. You might have to pursue some further reading on the subject as you start to build up your knowledge base. Such reading may be necessary as you start to prepare your slides and the content of your presentation.

- *Intellectual skills*
  - Depending on your academic year and level of study, most universities will require some form of intellectual skill in written and verbal assessments. Try and ensure that your knowledge and understanding are not purely descriptive. For example, many of our students on healthcare programmes may be asked to present on the topic of back pain as this is a common pain condition affecting many people. It would obviously be important to describe the anatomy, mechanisms and management of low back pain, but to really show you know and understand the subject you may need to delve deeper than just description. When presenting try to *discuss* and

analyse the wider evidence related to your specific topic. Different authors/researchers may present contradicting or similar findings to the investigations or management of low back pain. Many of the research studies or texts you read may all agree on a specific form of intervention for low back pain, so try and use *synthesis* to draw their conclusions together.

- The greater the grasp you have of the descriptive and intellectual aspects of your subject the more you will feel confident and in control. This will hopefully result in a higher grade, but most importantly it will reduce your public speaking fear. Questions will not be as daunting as before and an opportunity to share your knowledge and meet the examiner's or audience's needs.

Student Voices

Know the subject

'Trying to become more familiar with the subject to the point I feel confident to talk about it.'

'Identified in a peer-assisted learning (PAL) session that I feel less nervous when prepared and feel confident in knowledge.'

Keep it simple

> 'Everything should be made as simple as possible, but not simpler' (Albert Einstein, 1933)

This well-known and frequently used quote from Einstein is a key strategy in authentic public speaking. Many people who do not fully know or understand their topic use jargon or a complicated way to explain concepts. In the SUBH workshops many students felt this was an important concept to understand, although quite challenging to implement. In simplifying your presentation, you should have mastery of the subject and in turn reduce your fear. The audience will be more receptive if they are able to understand your message. Keeping it simple is closely related to knowing your subject and your audience – important strategies that are further developed in this chapter.

Individual Activity

How do you see the link between knowing your subject and keeping it simple? Can you truly be authentic if you present material you do not fully understand?

When talking about a complex subject it is very easy to use terms that you do not fully understand, and hope that if you say them quickly enough the audience will not catch on or ask you tricky questions. As an academic I regret that at times I have used a few complicated or technical terms that I did not fully understand or explain properly to the audience. Explaining complex concepts in a manner and language that are user friendly should be your aim in public speaking to get the audience onside. It is also important in enabling the audience to fully understand your message. Most importantly, it shows you fully know and understand your presentation topic. I have found that drowning the audience in technical language, and without fully explaining in simple terms, may have the following audience reactions:

- Members of the audience fall asleep.
- You lose the audience, they are no longer on your side.

- Audience lose interest in the topic and presentation as a whole.
- Some audience members may become frustrated and agitated.
- More use of mobile phones than usual by the audience.
- Negative body language from the audience.

The above audience reactions have happened to me in the past and I am sure may still occur again! Specifically, if I do not meet the audience needs and present the material in a way that they can understand. Apart from not meeting the audience needs, as a student who may have a fear of public speaking these negative audience reactions are bound to decrease your confidence. Have a look at the individual activity below that may help you become more tuned into audience reactions to an overcomplicated delivery!

Individual Activity

List a few of **the feelings you associate** with some of the above described audience reactions to an over-complicated presentation.

Do the above feelings to the audience reaction increase or decrease your public speaking fear?

If the audience does react negatively to an over-complicated presentation, the good news is that you can change this negative audience reaction and get them onside, resulting in a reduction of your fear.

Practical steps to apply this strategy to your public speaking

Next time you make a presentation, adopt the following steps. (Take note that some of these are further developed in other chapters and will be signposted.)

- *Less is more*
  - This is a starting point, when you are preparing your next presentation and following the above described steps in relation to knowing your subject.
  - Once you have gathered all your material and had a chance to absorb and understand it, think about how you could do one key thing:
    - Remove the excess, keep it lean: delete all the waffly, flowery, overly technical and repetitive language. If you could say something in one sentence, why use five?! Remember that most assessed presentations will have a time limit, so remove all the verbal flab and keep your presentation lean. When practising your presentation (Chapter 7) really try to say more in less time. This takes practice and the time to implement it in your presentation.
- *Keep it simple, not simplistic*
  - This is not easy, but what you should aim to do in all your presentations. This really shows that you know your subject. When I teach foot anatomy to level 1 university students I try my best to keep it as simple as possible. I obviously don't avoid anatomical terms like 'phalanges' (toes) or 'hallux' (big toe), but I do place them in context and use the lay term initially to help students understand. Some of the research methods and critical appraisal that I teach to students on evidence-based modules are full of jargon and complex terminology. In our teaching sessions we try to simplify some of that terminology and ensure it is linked to students' real-life examples, as well as relevant and not 'dumbed down'.

- Keep the structure
  - To keep it simple, do not forget the presentation structure. To avoid over-complication in your presentation and message, ensure your presentation is structured and flows from beginning to end. We will discuss structure (Chapter 5) and its importance in your presentation. Having a clear structure will add clarity and complement your simplified content.
  - Imagine if you spent all that time getting to grips with complex material and managed to present it in a simpler format, only to confuse the audience with a lack of structure.

Know your audience

Knowing your audience should be the starting point in your practice and preparation for any public speaking task. In business and marketing a lot of time and money goes into identifying a client/customer base and then aiming to meet the demands of the customer. In public speaking this should be no different, as with no public there would be no public speaking! In the first chapter we discussed that many fears are externally based and focused on the audience reaction to our speaking. A lot of fear related to public speaking would be reduced if we concentrated more on the audience and put them first.

In an assessed university presentation, you should have a clear idea what the examiners require and are expecting from you. As discussed previously, by reviewing the assessment guidelines you should know what the audience (examiners) need. Depending on your programme of study, you should aim to focus your presentation and message on what is relevant to your course of study. Most assessment guidelines will clearly state that your presentation should focus on the implications and relevance of your programme of study.

Practical steps to apply this strategy to your public speaking

Next time you make a presentation, adopt the following steps. As you can see from Figure 3.1, there is a strong relationship between each of the practical steps related to knowing your audience. (Note that some of these steps are further developed in other chapters and will be signposted.)

- *Who are my audience?*
  - If you do not prepare your presentation or public speaking task with the audience in mind, you may as well not even bother. When doing all the preparation and practice (see Chapter 7), and including your basics (Chapter 5), remember that who the audience are is key! Recently, I was the keynote speaker at a regional conference for peer support leaders at a university in the south-west of England. Before preparing and ultimately presenting the presentation, I made sure I gleaned as much information as possible about who the attendees were. Although it's impossible to know everything about an audience, the important information might cover the following:
    - Peers: are the audience members in your year of study or doing similar subjects/programmes of study? Do they have a grasp of the subject you are presenting, has it been covered at university?
    - Lecturing or other staff: presume if lecturing staff that they should have an idea about the subject you are presenting. Other staff may need more information on the basics of the subject and this would influence the content.
    - Lay audience: if you are presenting or speaking to a non-university or subject-aware audience, then it is important to deliver content that they would understand and align with. If you were a student ambassador and were welcoming potential students and parents at an open day, you would pitch your presentation accordingly.
- What do they want?
  - Depending on who the audience are, this will influence the information or message they may want to receive. If as described above your audience are parents and potential students at an open day, your presentation message would be related to the facilities at the university, and info on the programme of study. If your presentation was on a specific topic selected by your examiners, then your message would be clearly related to this requirement. Although this may seem obvious, many students do not fully absorb or read the requirements

and subject matter in their presentation guidelines. You may have a fantastic presentation but on the wrong subject, so unfortunately you will not have given the audience (examiners) what they want!

- How do they want it?
    - As discussed above, read the presentation guidelines for the format and structure of formal assessed presentations. If your public speaking is in other contexts really give a lot of thought to who your audience are and what they want. This section links in well with not only knowing your subject but also keeping it simple. Most audiences want to understand and grasp a topic easily, without having to do too much work. Using language and terms that a lay or professional audience are familiar with is fundamental to meeting the needs of your audience.

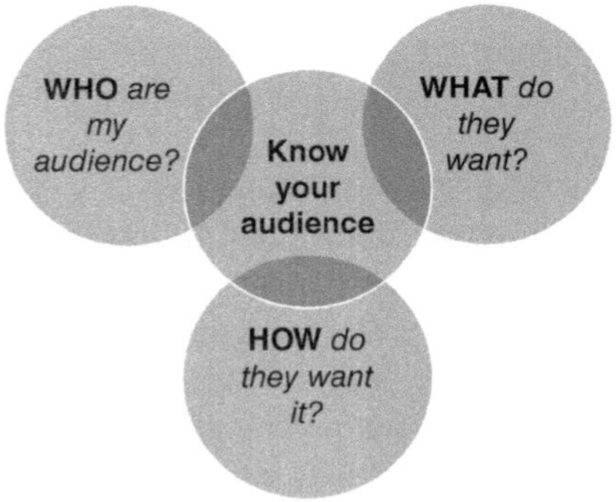

Figure 3.1 Know your audience

Tell stories

One of the opening slides in the three-hour SUBH workshops is a picture of a biscuit. The participants (audience) often look up at this slide and then me with a level of puzzled amusement. They signed up to a workshop on public speaking, not a baking course! The biscuit slide is a prompt to a story related to an awkward experience I had in public speaking which goes as follows:

As academics we often have to attend field boards to review the marks for our respective modules. Due to my stammer there are certain words that I really struggle with, which I am often able to replace with another suitable word. However, when it comes to reading out lists of student names on the field board I cannot change a Rebecca to a George to avoid the inevitable stammer. Further to this I cannot change my name to one that I would not stammer on; a well-known aspect of being a stammerer is stammering on your own name. When my turn came to introduce myself by name, I said RRob before eventually saying my name. Seconds later, one of my colleagues burst out into a chuckle as he thought I had my mouth full of biscuit.

This brief story had an immediate effect and could also be applied to your public speaking in the following ways:

- *Get the audience on your side*
    - Telling a story related to something you did or witnessed is a powerful tool which allows the audience to gain insight into you as a person. If in the process of telling the story the audience learn something personal about you, they then become invested in you and what you have to say. This in turn increases the interest factor in your presentation/public speaking which will make the whole process less stressful. Telling stories may sometimes allow the audience a glimpse of your vulnerability (Chapter 2), which as we have discussed is a key aspect of being an authentic public speaker.
- *Great way of introducing the main topic of the presentation/workshop*
    - In the case of the biscuit story, the fear and associated issues that may be related to public speaking were addressed early in the presentation. This story was an original way of opening the presentation and clearly introducing the topic. It hopefully whetted the audience's appetite and they wanted to find out more, and importantly as the presenter I was meeting the needs of the audience.

The literature on presentation skills and public speaking is littered with the benefits of stories and storytelling in public speaking.

There are many texts available that will give you in-depth information on using stories in your presentations. This is beyond the scope of the book, but hopefully this section will start you off in your storytelling journey. Let's explore a few practical steps to including stories in your authentic public speaking.

Practical steps to apply this strategy to your public speaking

- *Make the story relevant and to the point*
  - When using stories, it is vital to ensure that they are relevant and related to your topic. Is there a central theme or message in your story? Stories are a great way to introduce the topic and address concepts in a different way. Let's say your topic of discussion is on healthy eating and exercise to prevent obesity. You could give a long explanation of the varying food types, pros and cons of carbohydrates, fats and a detailed exercise programme, or tell a story of how someone or yourself reduced their weight through healthy eating and exercise. This type of story is really a case study but will give a clear indication of the benefits of diet and exercise based on a real-life event. This is something that many in the audience can identify with and appreciate. If you do use this type of storytelling that involves other people, change names and ensure that confidentiality is maintained. Also ensure that your story is relevant and succinct and that you get to the point quite quickly. Nothing will put an audience off more than a long rambling story that has no relevance whatsoever to the topic in hand.
- *Not just about me*
  - Stories can help the audience understand where you are coming from, and as already mentioned will get them on your side. However, try to avoid making yourself the central character in all your stories! Relate stories to the evidence, experiences of other colleagues, organisations or events that are not just connected to you. In doing this you also show the breadth aspect of storytelling and how this could relate to your topic and further understanding. One of the strategies (Chapter 4) we discuss is about our role as the messenger in public speaking and that it is 'not just about me'.

- *Beginning, middle and end*
  - In the same way a traditional story has a beginning, middle and an end, use this format in your public speaking. Let's say your presentation is on homelessness in major cities. Apart from giving the facts and figures on homelessness, you could highlight homelessness in a story format. At the beginning of the story you could outline some of the issues an individual or individuals may have had that resulted in them becoming homeless. The middle of the story could include the struggles and experiences of being homeless. Unless you have been homeless yourself, this could come from newspapers or personal accounts you have read or interviews with homeless people. The end of the story could relate to the outcomes of the individual/s being homeless and what society could do about prevention and support for homeless people.
- *Inspire audience engagement, and how you tell them*
  - Using a story may actively engage your audience, especially if it is on a topic they can identify with. Apart from the topic, how you tell the story is essential. This is closely related to all the aspects we discussed about being authentic. If you just rattle off a story, with no conviction or passion, you might just as well have not begun to tell it. The audience will want to see that you care, and that this story has some meaning and relevance, if not for you then for your topic and/or the audience. How you tell them applies to jokes and stories! Try the individual activity below to get you started in thinking about and devising a story for your next presentation or public speaking task.

Individual Activity

Do you have any upcoming presentations or public speaking tasks that you think would be suited to include a story?

Write the beginning, middle and end of a relevant story below.

What is the key message you are trying to convey?

Creativity

Creativity is not just about being good at art or coming up with ideas and innovations that no one else has done before. Creativity is a way of thinking and approaching tasks in a different way that can be applied to all walks of life. Creativity can also be thought of as taking risks as this approach may not always achieve the desired results. Creativity and originality in public speaking will allow you to be yourself and ultimately an authentic public speaker. In writing this book and presenting SUBH workshops I have always discussed different ways of being creative in public speaking.

Student Voice

Visual cues and authentic approach

'I spent a long time putting together my slides, and making sure there were a lot of visuals and visual cues that not only

kept eyes off me, but also prompted me to be more authentic and keep track.

I think it was one of those learning from this situation where I tried to fit too much in one presentation which I think I'd know from now on to reduce. But it was good to have a visual structure to fall back on, and your words of being authentic and not worrying about perfection stayed with me throughout.'

Practical steps to apply this strategy to your public speaking

In Chapter 5 we discuss some of the ways to be creative in relation to IT audiovisual slides, so there may be a small overlap in some of the practical ways to implement this strategy below.

- *Imagine you are in the audience*
    - I am sure you have been part of a presentation that has been boring and uninspiring? A presentation that is purely text based might easily put you to sleep! Death by PowerPoint (Chapter 5) is very common, where the presenter has basically filled all the slides with text and then proceeds to read these off word for word. Are they showing their knowledge, interest and passion for the subject?! Anyone could read their presentation instead of creatively delivering it to the audience.
- *Mix it up!*
    - Depending on the audience I am presenting to and what the subject is, I try to mix up the delivery of the content. In the SUBH workshops and my everyday public speaking/teaching, I use one or a combination of the following:
        - Graphics and pictures: fill each slide with a graphic or picture, maybe include a few key words. This will allow you to speak more freely and avoid the temptation of reading off the presentation slide.
        - Speech bubbles and animation: if using text, putting key points in a speech bubble prevents overcrowding the text. If you have a lot to say text wise (but avoid if possible) then put in bullet points and animate, so that only the relevant text appears as you speak.

- Stories: as already mentioned in this chapter, these are a great way to change the delivery of your content.
- Quotes and analogies: as used above, the Einstein quote in relation to simplicity in complex concepts and knowledge is a useful one and increases understanding of the concept. Analogies can also help get your point across to an audience. In relation to public speaking being a skill that must be learned and practised, this is not something that we can or cannot do. I often compare it to other skills (painting, surfing, etc.) in that we are not automatically good at these – they take practice. Quotes and analogies add another dimension to how you deliver information and concepts in your presentation.
- The odd video: in the SUBH workshops we use three short videos (4–5 minutes) that emphasise or reinforce certain information, and are also a great resource for self-directed learning.
- Post-its: when getting audiences to interact or share information Post-its are a great and imaginative resource. You could ask the audience to put down some ideas on a Post-it and share these with the person next to them. This is a technique I use a lot in teaching to get the students involved and interacting in the session. It is a great 'low-tech' method that does not require expensive IT equipment.
- Props: in my anatomy teaching there are lots of online apps and anatomy resources that students can use. I use anatomical models in a quiz format to revise or complement what is being covered. Recently, in a lecture for around 90 students, I asked them to bring an example of a research study that they could critically appraise related to their clinical practice, instead of just listening to me talking. In your next presentation you might try bringing along a prop or something representing the main subject you are discussing, as this will draw the audience's attention.

o Being creative in your public speaking takes a fair amount of thought and preparation, but will pay dividends in the end. It also allows the audience to be more involved in the process and respond positively to your public speaking. This should make you enjoy the experience and hopefully reduce your fear. Public speaking should always aim to get the audience involved either overtly, by verbally responding, or covertly/internally, by being mentally involved and immersed in what you have to say.

- Creativity does come more easily to some people, but with a bit of effort and thinking outside the box it is more than possible. In the practice chapter (Chapter 7) we will go over some more ideas and methods to practise creatively for public speaking. Being creative does have risks in that it may backfire, but most of the time the audience will thank you for making that extra effort. It is easy to trot out the same delivery method, time after time, so thinking outside the box shows that you care about your audience.

Chapter summary

This chapter has reviewed the following tried and tested strategies to become an authentic public speaker, namely know your subject, keep it simple, know your audience, tell stories and creativity. Not all of these strategies may appeal to you, but even using one or two will be of value to you as an authentic public speaker. Although most of the emphasis in this chapter is on presentations, the strategies covered can be applied to any public speaking activity at university from seminars to extra-curricular activities. Finally, I would advise you to complete the reflective space at the end of this chapter on the strategies to be authentic that we have covered.

Reflective Space

Using this reflective space will give you an opportunity to review and consolidate what has been covered in this chapter. This might be something that you have not done much of but, in in my experience and those of students in the SUBH workshops, it has proven to be really helpful.

Which of the strategies to be authentic (and also reduce your fear) could you use tomorrow? Why do the strategies you have chosen appeal to you?

- Know your subject
- Keep it simple
- Know your audience
- Tell stories
- Creativity

4

Strategies to be Authentic – Part Two

Specifically related to you the public speaker

OVERVIEW

This chapter will build on the previous chapter on strategies to become an authentic public speaker and help reduce the fear. All of the strategies in this chapter have been tried and tested in our SUBH workshops, with most students finding at least two or more of help in reducing their fear of public speaking. Most of the strategies in this chapter are more directly related to you as a public speaker. As discussed earlier, public speaking refers to any speaking task involving standing up and speaking to people. Most of the emphasis in this chapter is on presentations, but can be related to any public speaking activity including seminars, peer support, and clinical or work placements.

While reading through the strategies, please always have at the forefront of your mind that to really get to grips with these strategies, become a more authentic public speaker and reduce your fear you need to *practise*. We will be covering this later in the chapter specifically related to the varied ways of practising your public speaking (Chapter 7).

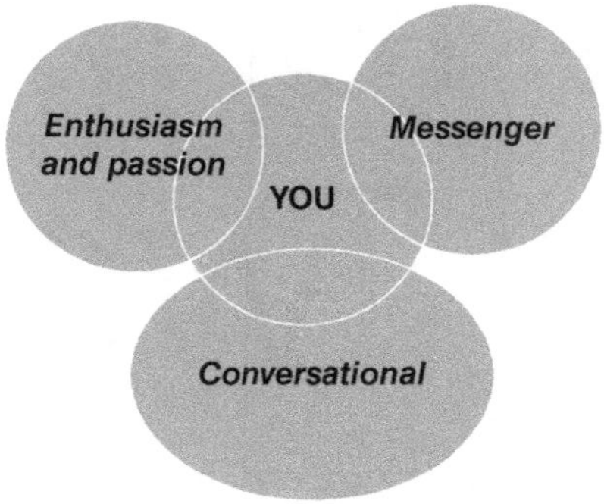

Figure 4.1 Strategies specifically focusing on you, the public speaker

Before we start it would be a good idea to jot down a few strategies in the individual activity below that you have used previously in relation to a presentation or public speaking in general. We use this activity with the students on the SUBH workshop, and like them I am sure you will find it useful in respect of what you do now and how you can change your public speaking practice.

Individual Activity

Which strategies have you used for a fear of public speaking or think may be useful?

Enthusiasm and passion

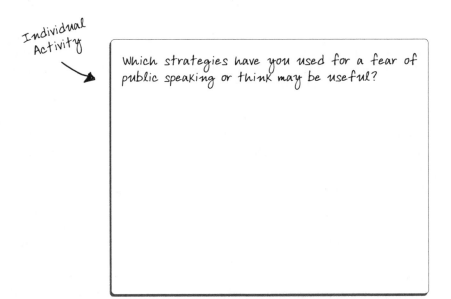

Enthusiasm and passion are the common characteristics highly valued by students when they positively evaluate teaching. Grabbing the topic by the scruff of the neck and making it come alive with your enthusiasm and passion ignites audience interest. If I receive positive feedback from students on my teaching, it is normally related to my enthusiasm and passion for the subject I am teaching. We have already stressed the importance of knowing your subject in public speaking; however, all the knowledge in the world would be of little use if the audience were bored senseless or fast asleep! One of the points that I stress in the SUBH workshops is that if we as presenters look bored, or show little passion or care for our subject, how can we expect an audience to care? Audiences will often invest their own time to listen to us, and therefore showing a genuine interest in our topic is the least we can do!

Importantly, showing enthusiasm and passion in public speaking is not the same as performing in public. Enthusiasm and passion are more about how we deliver and present ourselves to the audience. As the focus has been on being an authentic public speaker, we are all different personality wise and some of us may naturally be more introverted. Your enthusiasm and passion levels should feel right for you and not be an over-exaggerated version of how you express yourself. An audience will soon register and appreciate whether you are showing an interest in the topic or are just going through the motions. As previously discussed, your fear and enjoyment of public speaking are closely related to getting the audience on your side.

A positive outcome in being absorbed in your topic and passionately discussing it with your audience is that you do not have enough time to be fearful. I can recall when I started drifting away from a topic, thinking about how the talk was going and not being in the moment – that was when the fear and doubts started to creep in. As soon as I focused on what I was saying, and not how I was saying it, and became enthusiastic and passionate about the topic and sharing it, the fear began to disappear! And aside from this, the time flew by for both myself and the audience.

If we talk in public about a subject that really interests us, this makes the task of being enthusiastic and passionate a lot easier. For example, you might be involved in a student athletics society and asked to share your experience of running your first marathon. This is an achievement you are very proud of and enthusiasm for the topic would come naturally. On the other hand, your evidence-based module assessment may involve critically appraising the evidence in relation to a recent theory or paradigm in your programme of study. Although you are enjoying your academic programme, you may not relish trawling through numerous published studies and critically appraising their individual quality.

Try the individual activity below in relation to public speaking on a topic you are initially not really that interested in. This is a very useful exercise, as I am sure on some occasions you will be asked to speak in public about a topic that is of little interest to you, but may be of interest to your audience.

Individual Activity

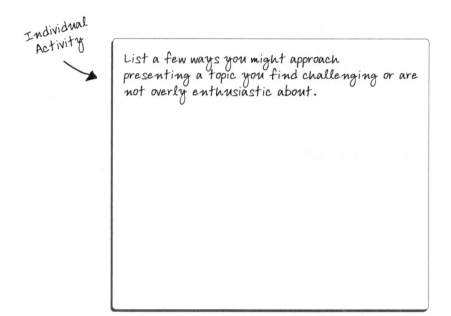

List a few ways you might approach presenting a topic you find challenging or are not overly enthusiastic about.

Practical steps to apply this strategy to your public speaking

Next time you make a presentation, I propose you adopt the following steps. (Note that some of these steps are further developed in other chapters and will be signposted.)

- *Bring the subject to life for you*
    - Further to the previous strategies discussed in this chapter, enthusiasm and passion occur when you bring the topic of your public speaking to life. What does this subject *mean to you* the presenter, how does it *impact* on your educational experience, personal life

or programme of study? What is the *relevance* of the topic to your studies and future career? By personalising and caring about the subject, this would make it easier to authentically show enthusiasm and passion.

- *Bring the subject to life for the audience*
  - If you have been asked to give a presentation in an area that you find challenging or holds no interest, then you will need to remove yourself from the equation. Turn it around and put more attention than usual on the audience.
  - What is the *relevance* of the topic to them, how could it be of *interest* and *use* to the audience? By showing a genuine interest in meeting the needs of the audience you will show your passion and enthusiasm.

See yourself as the messenger

Contrary to what we feel about public speaking it is not all about ourselves, the people doing the public speaking. Many texts on public speaking focus on the speaker with a lot of emphasis on how to speak, react to questions, adopt postures and a host of other public speaking skills. This study guide is guilty of this to an extent, but it is important that we move away from focusing solely on the speaker.

In the SUBH workshops, one of the more popular strategies is that of taking the focus off you the speaker and concentrating on what you are saying, i.e. your message. A previous text on public speaking (Souter, 2011) advises the speaker to see themself as a messenger, as part of the process and not actually the process itself. I have further developed this concept and it is one of the key strategies that resonates for students who have a fear of public speaking. It is also a strategy for people who have a stammer or speech dysfluency, who often feel that the audience are focusing purely on them and how they are speaking.

As soon as we start to discuss the concept of seeing oneself as a messenger, students who have a fear of public speaking often comment that this concept has changed their whole outlook on public speaking. In the first chapter we saw that many of the student fears associated with public speaking were external and associated with how audiences viewed speakers. The practical steps listed below will help you to see and operate in the speaking situation in a different way that will reduce the pressure and fear associated with public speaking.

Practical steps to apply this strategy to your public speaking

Audiences are there to hear your message, not just you!

This is a fantastic starting point for any public speaking or presentation you give as a student or public speaker in general. The only exception would be if you had a cult or celebrity following who are there to absorb your every word, regardless of its merits. For us average mortals, most audience members are there to hear what we have to say and not primarily to focus on us as the individual giving the presentation. In the SUBH workshop we discuss some of the work done by Pearson (2007), who as a life and NLP coach working with clients with a fear of public speaking for over 20 years, identified one of the three main categories of fear as 'It's all about me'.

Always try to remember and say to yourself before a presentation, that *the audience focus is primarily on what you have to say and not on how you say it.*

Change your attitude and reduce your fear

Start to view your role in public speaking differently. Changing this fundamental approach to public speaking will make a big difference to how you view the public speaking task. The result is that you will be more in control of your public speaking fear and looking forward to sharing your message. The focus is not on you, and although many students may feel this, you are not being judged by the audience – they are there to hear what you have to say.

Be conversational

Many of us can hold a conversation with a friend or someone we do not know and not give it much thought, but as soon as we are placed in front of an audience that ability to speak in public diminishes or becomes a fearful task. As with the messenger strategy that required a change in how we think about public speaking, the same goes for being conversational. Put yourself in the audience's shoes by trying the individual activity below regarding public speaking style.

Individual Activity

If you are part of an audience, which speaking style do you prefer – the formal rigid approach or a more fluid conversational style?

This conversational approach is widely discussed, covered in public speaking TED Talks, written about by many in relation to public speaking, and also well received by students in the SUBH workshops. According to Branham and Pearce (1996) modern public speaking uses a conversational approach that is inclusive, includes the audience, and is supported by contemporary public speaking texts for undergraduate courses. In a recent paper on the historical view of the teaching of public speaking, the current personal conversational style has ensured more connection between audience and speaker (Bailey, 2019). Interestingly, some earlier evidence by Motley and Molloy (1994) found that by being more communication orientated (i.e. sharing the information and message with the audience, conversational) as opposed to a performance orientation (a formal and 'flawless delivery') appeared to reduce public speaking anxiety in students. The above evidence shows a further reason to adopt a conversational approach in your public speaking. This conversational approach fits in well with many of the strategies and the overall emphasis on being an authentic public speaker.

When standing up in front of an audience there are a few practical ways in which you can be conversational in your manner and delivery.

Practical steps to apply this strategy to your public speaking

- *Conversational mindset*
    - Very simply, every time you are about to speak in public, regardless of the number of people in the audience, approach the task as if you are going to have a conversation with them. This would immediately mean that you are speaking to and with the audience and not at them. You are including them in the process and they would in turn be more responsive to you and your message.
- *Conversational approach in action*
    - Imagine you are speaking to a group of friends and having a conversation, and then translate this to an audience and use the same approach to be conversational. You will notice how the seven points below link in and have a lot in common with the strategies we discussed to be an authentic public speaker. Hopefully you would do the following:

- Maintain eye contact and not look away from them: when speaking to someone, you would hopefully maintain eye contact. Use the same approach with an audience; try and maintain eye contact throughout and avoid looking away or out of the window. Eye contact can be achieved by briefly looking at each audience member for 3–5 seconds as you visually scan the room. Remember that you are have having a conversation with many people, so try not to focus on just one person.
- Be in the moment: when speaking to someone all your attention would be on them and in the present speaking situation, and like the audience they would soon catch on that you wanted to be somewhere else. At that present moment your conversational partner and the audience deserve all your attention.
- Speak in a language and use terms they could understand: in your everyday conversation you would hope that the people you are speaking to get your message and understand what you are speaking about. This is dependent on the people we are speaking to (know your audience), and therefore we would ensure that the language we use is at the right level. When speaking to academic colleagues in relation to recently published research on any subject, I would use a different language and technical terms from those used in conversation with a lay person or non-researcher for instance. The same applies to speaking to an audience. Keep it simple and user friendly, otherwise you will lose that audience quite quickly.
- Try not to bore them and get to the point: I am sure you can remember being in a conversation when the other person rambled on and on with no regard for your resultant lack of interest. In the same way, many audiences get bored (I am sure you have been in the past – I have) if the speaker does not keep their presentation concise and to the point, so try to have some structure and ensure you focus on key points to keep your audience awake.
- Show some passion and enthusiasm in the conversation: in the same way that a rambling, boring conversation will lose

your interest, so too will a speaker who looks disinterested. In conversations and public speaking, a speaker's attitude will play a big part in a successful outcome. If the speaker shows enthusiasm and passion for the speaking task, the audience will be more in tune with the presentation.

- Remember that a conversation is a two-way process: most conversations involve interaction from those who converse, otherwise it is not a conversation. In public speaking, with you standing up front, this can be a bit more challenging. When teaching or giving a lecture I always ensure that I have some sort of interaction with the audience in the form of questions or asking them to think about a certain scenario or example. Some speakers use interactive slides that the audience can respond to via their smartphones. In this way they are getting the audience on board straight away. If you are giving a presentation as part of a module assessment, it can be quite difficult to ask the examiners a bunch of questions directly. You could on the other hand ask open-ended questions and for the audience to reflect on these without expecting a direct answer. By involving the audience you will get the most from your presentation, and in many ways you will be doing something that many public speakers don't do – connect with their audience.
- Pause and reflect: in a conversation, apart from finishing sentences, there are also natural pauses and sometimes moments of reflection. As a speaker who is fearful and not in the moment, you may want to get your presentation over as quickly as possible. Try to pause and let what you have said sink in and be absorbed by the audience. They will often respect you more if you speak without rushing and are able to pause when you choose to do so, on your own terms. This shows that you are in control and able to maintain your authentic public speaking self.

o From the points above in relation to the conversational approach to public speaking, I would encourage you to work through the individual activity below to really get to grips with conversational public speaking.

Individual Activity

How can you put the seven points in the **conversational approach** to public speaking into action for your next public speaking task?

1. What is your topic?
2. Who are your audience?

Avoid being nervous about your nervousness

The final strategy in relation to becoming an authentic public speaker, which will help you control or reduce your fear of public speaking, is harnessing the awareness that you may be nervous. This awareness is closely aligned with being authentic and fully acknowledging your vulnerability as a person and a public speaker.

This is a simple strategy that is briefly described by Ni (2016) in the phrase 'avoid being nervous about your nervousness', and using that nervous energy in a positive way. I have expanded on the above strategy by outlining some practical steps at the end of this section that you can use in your public speaking.

In Chapter 1 we discussed how a fear of public speaking is common amongst students and the general population. It is in this light that you should always approach your public speaking task and be aware that this nervousness is normal. As an experienced university lecturer, whose day job involves public speaking, I am not immune from feelings of nervousness and some of the physical ‘fight or flight’ symptoms (sweating, blushing, increased heart rate, etc.) that are normal healthy reactions and prepare us for action.

Student Voices

Strategies that are effective

‘The strategies we considered have continued to ease my anxieties. For example, I find being aware of my anxiety has made a huge difference and acknowledging that others have similar worries has also been a massive support. It’s completely normal to feel nervous and anxious during presentations and group discussions – we are only human. I learnt that practice and perseverance make perfect, so I’m not giving up just yet!’

Many writers on public speaking emphasise that we should accept the fact that we will be nervous when about to do public speaking. In the SUBH workshops, students respond well to this idea of being fully aware and acknowledging this normal response to public speaking. Given that such a high percentage of the student population and public have a fear of public speaking as discussed earlier in this book, it is therefore not surprising and quite normal for us to feel the same. Even after my many years of teaching and public speaking, I often feel nervous initially before I start speaking in public.

Student Voices

Strategies that are effective

‘The main things for me are although I still feel nervous (my HR at least doubles!) I’m not nervous about my nervousness.

Also, I find that by making sure I know my subject well, I naturally become more passionate about it, and peers have said my confidence and presentation skills have improved drastically!’

Practical steps to apply this strategy to your public speaking

Before you are about to speak in public, the following steps might help you in relation to being fully aware of your fear and nervousness:

- *Breathe and do something physical*
  - When public speaking, it is amazing how often we forget to breathe or increase our breathing rate when feeling anxious or in the 'fight or flight' response. When we are stressed, our breathing becomes shallow and fast, and stems from the chest, not the diaphragm or abdomen region (Consolo et al., 2008). Our aim is to slow our breathing down, become more aware of it, and change to relaxed deep breathing, technically known as diaphragmatic breathing. This relaxed deep breathing will not only reduce our stress levels and control our breathing, but may also help in projecting our voices (see Chapter 7 on breathing exercises).
  - Apart from concentrating on your breathing, go for a brief stroll and do something physical; avoid vegetating in a static state in a corner somewhere before your presentation. Physical exercise is well known for increasing levels of the feel good/happiness hormones such as endorphins, dopamine and serotonin. I am not advocating you do an intense workout or run just before you stand up and be heard to achieve the 'runners high'. Just being active will increase your feeling of wellbeing before you start speaking in public.
- *Recognise your nervousness as normal*
  - Although it is not pleasant to feel nervous before we speak in public, as discussed above, embrace and acknowledge your nervousness. If you view this as a normal occurrence, which affects most people who speak in public, you will be able to manage it more and use this nervousness in a positive way.
- *Positive nervous energy*
  - A bit of nervousness will keep you on your toes and bring out the best in you. If you are too laid back, do no preparation and give it minimal thought beforehand, there is a good chance your public speaking will suffer. Use that nervous energy positively

as the fuel for your enthusisaian and passion in your impending public speaking task. Public speaking is tiring, and you will need to get your fuel from somewhere!

Chapter summary

This chapter has built on the previous chapter in reviewing strategies to become an authentic public speaker and help reduce your fear. Most of the reviewed strategies are directly related to you as a public speaker, namely: enthusiasm/passion, see yourself as the messenger, be conversational and avoid being nervous about your nervousness. These strategies have been very positively evaluated by students, mainly because they are a different way of approaching public speaking. I use these strategies all the time when I teach and receive positive feedback. I am sure you will benefit from being conversational and not letting the inevitable nervousness get in the way of your public speaking. Finally, please do not forget to complete the reflective space at the end of this chapter that focuses on strategies directly related to you as a public speaker.

Reflective Space

Using this reflective space will give you an opportunity to review and consolidate what has been covered in this chapter. This might be something that you have not done much of, but in in my experience and those of students in the SUBH workshops, it has proved really helpful.

Reflect on which of the strategies to be authentic (and also reduce your fear) you could use tomorrow. Why do the strategies you have chosen appeal to you?

- Enthusiasm/passion
- See yourself as the messenger
- Be conversational
- Avoid being nervous about your nervousness

5

Remember the Basics

OVERVIEW

The previous chapters focus on specific strategies to be an authentic public speaker, which should help you to reduce your fear of public speaking. Although the focus is on becoming an authentic public speaker, it is important that we do not forget the basics that can make our speaking task, i.e. a presentation, a lot more stressful and reduce unnecessary fear. This chapter is set out as a chronological checklist with specific details outlined for the action or tasks that are not self-explanatory. There will be a bit of repetition, as some of the material will be discussed more fully in other chapters in the book, and these chapters will be signposted. As mentioned in the SUBH workshops, a bit of repetition is not always detrimental as it helps to reinforce our learning and remember some key points.

I would strongly advise you to make sure that you have read through, ticked off and completed each action or task before your presentation. This chapter checklist will help you focus on the basics before and during your presentation. Ignoring the tried and tested basic actions/tasks could unnecessarily increase your fear when this could be avoided. Some of the actions/tasks are covered in other chapters and this will be signposted.

I have encountered many students who are confident in public speaking but increase their stress level because they have overlooked the basics. For those who already have a fear of public speaking, missing some basic actions before and during a presentation will further increase that fear.

The basics: a chronological checklist

✓ *Tick each action/task* in the checklist once it is completed for each specific section that details before, during and after your presentation. Most of the actions/tasks are self-explanatory, although some will have further details below the checklist. Most of the actions/tasks outlined below are basics that are often neglected. The *actions/tasks listed are not basics, but are covered in more detail in other chapters; they are incorporated to show the whole picture. The entire Basics Chronological Checklist is included in the Appendix.

Day(s) before the presentation

Checklist

- ☐ Have you read the module assessment guidelines?
- ☐ *Have you practised your presentation (see Chapter 7)?
- ☐ Do you have a copy and backup of your presentation software (PowerPoint, Prezi, Slidebeam, Flowfella) on your USB or online (email, iCloud, etc.)?
- ☐ Have you checked that your presentation is easy to download onto a PC and is not faulty?
- ☐ Have you constructed your presentation slides effectively?
- ☐ Do you have a copy of your presentation slides or will you be using notes?
- ☐ Does the assessor/examiner require a copy of your PowerPoint/Prezi slides?

Further detail for some of the above checklist action/tasks

Have you read the module assessment guidelines?

This is always the starting point for your presentation preparation. You may have a fantastic presentation prepared and presented, but this is not much use if it's not on the assessment topic, does not meet the module learning outcomes, or ignores the timing or format instructions. This can cause you a lot of stress and anxiety if you get it wrong. I have often listened to a presentation with a tinge of regret when the student concerned has gone off piste and not fully answered the question or addressed the requested topic.

Have you checked that your presentation is easy to download onto a PC and is not faulty?

I would strongly advise that you have a copy of your presentation on a USB and not on your email account. Email is fine for backup but it can sometimes be time consuming or difficult to log into your email account. We have had instances where students were unable to log into their email and caused a delay for themselves and others in starting their presentations. The end result was increased stress and anxiety all round.

Have you constructed your presentation slides effectively?

A very common problem with many presentations is the ineffective designing and writing up of the presentation slides. In constructing the slides take note of the following:

- *Text* – Avoid the overuse of text on each slide and in general, as this will send any audience to sleep, and can make the presentation uninspiring and boring! An over-reliance on text also shows a lack of effort to an extent, as it is very easy to cut and paste loads of text onto a slide. If you are going to include text in bullet form, use key points and animate each bullet point so that you can discuss it as it appears on the screen. Remember to use a plain font that can be easily read and of sufficient size that the audience can read it. Using different colours to highlight a key point is advisable.
- *Graphics* – As you are using a visual aid, try and make it visual and not over-populated by text! 'A picture paints a thousand words' has a lot of truth to it. I often fill a slide with a graphic and then use some key words or phrases. Using boxes or shapes with key points is another useful visual technique.
- *Less is more* – Focus on the key points on each slide; do not cram each slide with graphs, tables, graphics and text.

Do you have a copy of your presentation slides or will you be using notes?

It's useful to have a paper copy of the presentation slides so that you know where you are in relation to the overall presentation, and this can help with your timing. I often convert my presentation slides to a handout with six slides per page to avoid having pages and pages of slides. Another option is to use cards with the key points numbered for each slide.

Night before and morning of the presentation

Checklist

- ☐ Did you have a good night's sleep the night before?
- ☐ Did you set the alarm clock or phone to wake up in time?
- ☐ Did you have your clothes laid out the night before?
- ☐ Apart from wearing appropriate clothing for the occasion, is this comfortable?
- ☐ Hope you did not skip breakfast?
- ☐ Did you consider the traffic and how you will get to the university on time?
- ☐ Presume you have checked and know which room on campus your presentation is in?
- ☐ Have you had a toilet break before your presentation or know where the nearest toilet facilities are?
- ☐ Presume you arrived at the venue a good 30+ minutes before?
- ☐ Have you uploaded your presentation onto the PC, projector and university IT system with enough time to spare?
- ☐ Have you asked the IT or academic staff if you are not sure where to upload your presentation?
- ☐ Presume you have checked that the presentation is correctly projected onto the screen?
- ☐ If you are using any online links to websites or resources, have you ensured the links are working before your presentation starts?

Further detail for some of the above checklist actions/tasks

Did you have a good night's sleep the night before?

Public speaking can be quite tiring regardless of whether you fear it or not. It's really important to get a good night's sleep, although it's difficult to recommend an exact figure in hours, but you should know how much you need to feel refreshed the following day.

If you go 'out on the town' the night before or get to bed in the early hours, I would strongly contest your ability to successfully speak in public. Even though you may be nervous the night before, and find it difficult to get to sleep, going to bed early is highly recommended. We all have an optimal level of sleeping hours to enable us to function properly and be refreshed for the day ahead. My stammer and ability to speak confidently and enjoy public speaking is greatly affected by the amount of sleep I have the night before. Normally seven hours will do the trick for me, but sometimes this is not possible due to prior evening engagements or difficulty in getting to sleep.

Apart from wearing appropriate clothing for the occasion, is this comfortable?

Normally, for an assessed presentation, students are often required to dress smart casual (follow the presentation guidelines). Something that is often neglected is the comfort factor. If you never wear a tie or smart high-heeled shoes (unless specified to do so) avoid doing so at all costs. You need to feel comfortable in your clothing, as this can make a real difference in your presentation.

Presume you arrived at the venue a good 30+ minutes before?

In my 16+ years of teaching and public speaking, nothing causes a rise in my stress and anxiety levels more than turning up late for a presentation, with minimal time to set up. As in the actions/tasks below, it is absolutely vital that you give yourself enough time to log on to the PC, upload your presentation, and check that the projector and IT equipment is working. Sometimes this will be done for you beforehand, but not always.

Presentation is about to start

Checklist

- ☐ If using a pointer or remote slide control, have you plugged it in and does it work?
- ☐ Have you remembered your notes or prompt cards?
- ☐ Do you have a bottle of water or something to drink if needed?

- ☐ Have you taken enough breaths if you feel the nervousness about to start?
- ☐ Where and how are you standing in the room?
- ☐ *Have you taken on board the nonverbal information (Chapter 6) in this study guide?
- ☐ Any thoughts about the audience?
- ☐ How will you start your presentation?
- ☐ *Have you followed the strategies to be an authentic speaker (see Chapter 3 and 4)?
- ☐ *Are you still taking into account the nonverbal information and acting on it (Chapter 6)?
- ☐ Is there a clear structure to your presentation?
- ☐ Have you followed the timing guidelines and made sure you are sticking to your allocated time?
- ☐ Are you using your presentation slides effectively?
- ☐ Presume you are clear on how you will end your presentation?
- ☐ Are you prepared for questions and have you thought about how to answer them?

Further detail for some of the above checklist actions/tasks

Where and how are you standing in the room?

Are you hidden behind the podium or PC, with your face and gaze on the screen, or out in front where you and the audience can see each other? So often students hide behind the podium and avoid really looking at the audience; instead they are reading from the PC screen. Sometimes, students may be standing in front but are turned away from the audience and basically reading from the projector screen on the wall behind them. It's fine to occasionally glance at the screen or use your infra-red/laser pointer to point out material.

**Have you taken on board the nonverbal information (Chapter 6) in this study guide?*

Apart from the nonverbal material covered in Chapter 6, the non-verbal take-home message is to ensure there is a congruency between your verbal and nonverbal self! Nothing is more off-putting than a presenter whose verbal message is given away nonverbally. If you verbally state enthusiasm and passion for some aspect of your presentation, then hopefully this will be reflected in your demeanour and on your face.

Any thoughts about the audience?

With our fear of public speaking we often neglect the audience as we are so focused on ourselves and what we have to say. We are doing the public speaking but are speaking to an audience (public), hence the term 'public speaking'. It's important to ensure that you are meeting the needs of the audience and that you are delivering your presentation at a level that is suitable to the type of audience. (We discussed this more fully in Chapter 3.) Note that when you look at faces in the audience it is often easy to misinterpret signals. Often those faces can appear too serious or possibly disapproving, when in fact this is the facial expression of an intent listener.

How will you start your presentation?

The manner in which you start your presentation or public speaking task can set the scene and play a role in increasing or reducing your fear factor. Ensuring you have the basics right, and are standing in front of the audience having done all necessary practice and preparation, and having checked the PC/IT is working, always makes for a good start! If you are flustered because the PC/projector is malfunctioning, or your slides are not showing correctly, or you are still sorting out notes, you will be increasing your fear factor. Importantly, this sends out a negative message to the audience who you really want to be on your side right from the beginning. Strange as it may seem, the audience will want you to succeed.

First impressions often count in public speaking, and that is why the beginning is always important and can be quiet challenging at times.

An athlete does not normally sprint off from the blocks without doing an initial warm-up or preparation, and the same applies to presentations/public speaking. Most of the basic actions/tasks described in this chapter will ensure you are prepared and ready for your presentation. Before you enter the room take some steadying breaths and really start to focus your attention on 'being in the moment' (Chapter 3).

Some speakers are introduced beforehand but in most student presentations you would start the presentation. Personally, I always used to (and still do at times) struggle with introducing myself by name, as I often used to stammer when doing so. I have since used self-disclosure in the form of 'verbal housekeeping' which often initially left audiences a bit stunned, and amused at times, but really works for me (see Chapter 2). This is an unexpected opening but takes the pressure off me and gets the audience on side.

Here are a few considerations when starting your presentation:

- *Nonverbal* – How you stand in front of the audience and the nonverbal cues (see Chapter 6) you give off at the start can really set the scene for the rest of the presentation. In the earlier chapters we discussed the main approach of being authentic and being yourself. This is the fundamental approach we adopt for public speaking and a key approach for reducing your fear. However, there should be a balance between being authentic and your nonverbal self in public speaking. If you normally slouch around with your shoulders forward and head towards the ground, this would be a time to adopt a more upright posture. Be aware of your nonverbal behaviour as this can make or break your presentation (see Chapter 6).
- *Opening lines* – There is no set of opening lines or recipe for what you should say or not say at the start of your presentation. There has been much written about how to open a presentation or a speech, and while some is useful it may not be applicable to you. Many speakers introduce themselves, or sometimes thank the audience, or start with a question or a story, or set the scene. Any of these options are open to you, although students normally introduce themselves and give the title of their talk or inform the audience of their topic.

It might be *worth trying something a bit different*, although you should always be aware of the guidelines and expectations of your module examiners. Make sure your different opening is closely associated, and that it will enhance and lead on directly to your topic. Here are a few examples:

- *Start with a question* – If your presentation is on a specific musculo-skeletal condition (low back pain), you could throw a question out to the audience. *Is low back pain always associated with a poor posture?* This question is quite controversial as it has been thought that poor posture and low back pain are always related, but this is disputed. Another example question to get your audience thinking is: *If you injured your back six months ago and it is fully healed, why could you still be in pain?* This would lead on nicely to the challenge of chronic/long-term pain. The use of questions can also make your presentation more conversational (see Chapter 4).
- *Start with a story* – In my workshops, apart from starting with the 'verbal housekeeping', I put up a picture of a biscuit. This is the prompt for a story which is linked to the content of the SUBH workshop (see the full details on use of stories in public speaking in Chapter 3). Staying on the low back pain theme, you could briefly tell a story about a clinical case involving a patient (anonymous) who has chronic low back pain, and on whom all treatments have been ineffective. This could lead on to your definitions and understanding of the mechanisms of low back pain.

During the presentation

Checklist

- ☐ *Have you followed the strategies to be an authentic speaker (see Chapters 3, 4)?
- ☐ *Are you still taking into account the nonverbal information and acting on it (Chapter 6)?
- ☐ Is there a clear structure to your presentation?
- ☐ Have you followed the timing guidelines and made sure you are sticking to your allocated time?

- ☐ Are you using your presentation slides effectively?
- ☐ Presume you are clear on how you will end your presentation?
- ☐ Are you prepared for questions and have you thought about how to answer them?

Further detail for some of the above checklist actions/tasks

Is there a clear structure to your presentation?

As above make sure you have followed the guidelines and the format of your presentation. Structuring your presentation is a key skill that will show your understanding of the subject and clarity of thought. As in writing your coursework or dissertation there should be a beginning, middle and end (more commonly thought of as an introduction, discussion and conclusion). Think of your structure in three parts – two is too short and four might be too much.

Traditionally we often *begin* our presentation by stating the main aims or objectives of what we intend to cover (see above: 'How will you start your presentation?'). The *middle* usually consists of the bulk of the material we intend to present, while the *end* is the conclusion or overview of our presentation (See below: 'Presume you are clear on how you will end your presentation?'). Each section should hopefully lead on to the next and be related overall.

Have you followed the timing guidelines and made sure you are sticking to your allocated time?

This is when practice and preparation come to the fore (see Chapter 7). I have seen this happen on many occasions when a student has been given the one-minute left signal from the examiner, only to realise that they are only half way through their presentation. Resultant panic ensues, where the pace increases tenfold, slides are whizzed through, and the student is trying desperately to cram in the remaining material. The end result is increased fear and panic, and an overall low grade for the assessment.

While practising your presentation, it is always crucial that you verbalise and time your presentation (see Chapter 7), and this may take a few run-throughs to get it right. Also important is that you account for the increased vocal delivery that may occur in your assessed presentation, due to expected nervousness.

Are you using your presentation slides effectively?

Presentation slides are very effective visual aids that are commonly used and required for many presentations. The problem is that many students (and experienced presenters) do not use then effectively. The phrase 'death by PowerPoint' refers to their incorrect use, which can negatively affect your presentation. Common errors that I regularly see are as follows:

- *Reading out word for word* – Remember you are there to speak, give a presentation, and not read out all the slides in public. Many students often attach themselves to the podium and read out their presentations, practically word for word. This is enough to put most audiences to sleep, and is technically not public speaking, more like public reading.
- *Less is more* – Very easy to cram your slides into a presentation, so that you are rushing to finish in time. Important to have time to talk around a slide, which would allow your presentation to be more conversational.
- *Animated delivery* – Animation is a useful technique enabling key points to appear as you are about to discuss them. Be wary not to get carried away and animate everything, include spinning of text, whooshing and other sounds. This will detract from your message and what you are saying. I remember when I was a student many years ago and presentation software was quite new on the market. One of my fellow classmates decided to go to town with his newly acquired PowerPoint presentation software, by using every animation tool available with accompanying sounds. The result was a serious case of style over substance and much of the message and content was lost!

Presume you are clear on how you will end your presentation?

In the same respect that starting your presentation is important, so too is closing or concluding. The conclusion as discussed earlier can often be an overview and signpost to future actions or recommendations. The audience do not want to be dropped suddenly at the end, rather guided and made aware of the link between the beginning, middle and end. Questions are often left to the end and give the audience an opportunity to confirm or query certain aspects discussed in the presentation. In an assessed module presentation, questions are often asked by the examiners and sometimes by your fellow classmates.

Are you prepared for questions and have you thought about how to answer them?

Many students are terrified by questions during or after a presentation. In our SUBH workshops this is often noted as a fear or issue with public speaking.

This is mainly related to not being able to answer the question and appearing ignorant in front of peers. We will be discussing questions further (see Chapter 3) but it is important to make sure you know your material in depth and are able to answer the questions. If you do not know the answer, save time by not waffling or making something up which will only frustrate your examiners. This will then give the opportunity for the examiner to ask another question, which hopefully you will be able to answer.

After the presentation

Checklist

- ☐ Did you reflect on your presentation?
- ☐ Did you read the feedback from your examiner/s and reflect on how it could have been improved?

Further detail for some of the above checklist actions/tasks

Did you reflect on your presentation?

Once your presentation is over, give yourself a bit of time to reflect on it. There are many models of reflection in the literature that can be used as a guide. I would recommend you focus on *what you did, how you feel it went* and *how it could be improved*. I would also include some thoughts on your perceptions of the audience response. It is important not to be too hard on yourself if you feel it did not go as well as you hoped. One of the difficulties in self-reflection on public speaking is that it is sometimes difficult to gauge what the audience really thought of your presentation. On many occasions I have left after speaking in public, thinking that it did not go well, only to be given positive feedback later on.

Did you read the feedback from your examiner/s and reflect on how it could have been improved?

Did you just look at your mark and then not bother to read the rest of the written feedback on your presentation? It is really worthwhile reading that feedback even when you gain a high mark, as there is always room for improvement. And that goes for all of us, even with years of experience in public speaking. Did your self-reflection and the feedback match up?

Regardless of your overall grade, read the feedback and see how you could act on it to improve as a public speaker.

Student Voices

Various ways of covering the public speaking basics

'Be prepared way in advance so have plenty of time to go over everything.'

'I will rehearse as much as possible and be well prepared with my material, PowerPoint and prompt cards.'

'Having short notes.'

'Always bring a bottle of water.'

'Wearing something comfortable.'

'Once they are finished [presentations] I don't dwell on how they went.'

Chapter summary

The main aim of this study guide is for you to focus on becoming an authentic public speaker. However, as you can see from this chapter, it is important that you do not forget the basics that can make your speaking task, i.e. a presentation, a lot more stressful and reduce unnecessary fear. As discussed above, you may initially have minimal public speaking fear, but this may quickly change if you ignore the basics. At the end of this chapter, some students' voices commented on how they approached some of the basics in public speaking. These may be similar to how you approach some of the basics in public speaking. Finally, please try and complete the reflective space below, as this will consolidate your understanding and show the importance of the often-neglected basics in public speaking.

Reflective Space

Using this reflective space will give you an opportunity to review and consolidate what has been covered in this chapter. This might be something that you have not done much of, but in in my experience and those of students in the SUBH workshops, this has proved really helpful.

Reflect on what could you take home from this chapter in respect of the basics. Specifically:

Write down which of the basic actions/tasks you feel are essential.

Are there any additional actions or tasks that you could include?

Do you take the basics into account when speaking in public – any further thoughts?

6

Nonverbal Techniques

OVERVIEW

This chapter will build on the previous material covered with a focus on being an authentic public speaker in relation to nonverbal behaviour. Our verbal communication might be focused on being authentic but let down by our nonverbal communication. This chapter will enable you to become more authentic by ensuring you are aware of your nonverbal behaviour and consider ways to modify it accordingly. Trying to be authentic with possible conflicting nonverbal messages is a real challenge with no straightforward answer. We will endeavour to try and make sense of the challenge between authentic verbal and nonverbal communication. The main aim of this chapter is to make you consider your nonverbal communication when public speaking and how best to address it in a way that makes you feel comfortable. All the nonverbal techniques in this chapter have been discussed and positively reviewed by participants in the SUBH workshops, and have been of benefit in reducing public speaking fear.

Nonverbal communication includes posture, facial expression, gestures and cues given without the use of words. Nonverbal communication is a universal language that is understood by most of us, regardless of the language spoken. However, it is important to note that there are differences across cultures in nonverbal communication and that nonverbal behaviours can be better understood when viewed from a specific cultural perspective (Matsumoto and Hwang, 2016). This is a relevant factor to bear in mind, as in the current university climate, we have many international students and a diverse multicultural student population. On our SUBH workshops we have many students whose first language is not English, and this combined with cultural difference both verbally and nonverbally may present a challenge in public speaking.

In public speaking the audience will be taking cues and making assumptions (often incorrectly) about you long before you open your mouth to speak. Research has found that judgements on trustworthiness and competence amongst others were made from facial expressions after only a 100 millisecond exposure time (Willis and Todorov, 2006). Standing up and being heard means that, whether we like it or not, all eyes will be on us. Being the centre of attention was one of the real fears identified in Chapter 1 by many students that had a negative effect on their public speaking experience.

When speaking in public there is one key question to ask yourself and always remember in relation to nonverbal behaviour:

> *Are verbal and nonverbal communication in harmony (congruency) or about to tear each other apart?*

I cannot stress this point enough. To be authentic in public speaking you cannot ignore the nonverbal element. Most importantly, always ensure that what you say is reflected and mirrored in your behaviour. There is nothing more off-putting than having a speaker verbalise things but nonverbally send out a completely different message; e.g. a speaker who states at the beginning of a presentation that he is very pleased to be there, but his grim facial expression exudes the exact opposite. Immediately, the audience may become sceptical and not really trust the message or the speaker. One of the challenges in relation to verbal and nonverbal harmony is ensuring that what you say is clearly reflected in your body language. Congruency between verbal and nonverbal behaviour is stressed repeatedly in the SUBH workshops and its application to public speaking.

To start thinking about verbal and nonverbal harmony, a bit of reflection is a good place to begin as it can help you identify areas to work on. Try the individual activity below as it may help you become more aware of your nonverbal behaviour.

Individual Activity

Try and think of a few examples and write down when you have said one thing and your body has said another.

We will now discuss five nonverbal components of public speaking and practical tips to consider when you next stand up and be heard.

Appearance

Appearance matters in relation to public speaking and is closely linked to first impressions as discussed above. The idiom 'Don't judge a book by its cover' relates to making impressions about a person based solely on their appearance. Unfortunately many people (and that can include your audience) may be guilty of making a wrong judgement about you before you even say a word, so try and make life easier for yourself and pay attention to your appearance because if the audience give off negative vibes this will increase your stress levels. Appearance is related to the type of public speaking you will be involved in and who your audience are (Chapter 1 and Chapter 3).

Practical steps to consider

- *Dress and clothing*
    - When our students are involved in module presentation assessments, they normally go for smart casual dress. This is dependent on the requirements of the module and as a student you would normally be advised beforehand. If not, it would be a good idea to enquire about a dress code for your presentation. Turning up at a presentation in shorts and flip-flops may not be your smartest move if everyone else has followed a required smart casual dress code. If, on the other hand, you are giving a presentation related to surfing and the setting is on a beach to a group of surfers that is another matter. Who you are speaking to and in what context is fundamental to your dress code. Wearing the appropriate dress does show thought and preparation for the speaking task ahead.
    - Apart from dressing up for the occasion, I always stress the importance of clothing comfort in the SUBH workshops. Let's say

you are asked to dress smart casual for your presentation, and you don't normally wear a suit or smart narrow shoes. On the day itself, that suit is uncomfortable, and the tight-fitting shoes are giving you blisters! Do you think this choice of clothing is beneficial to your public speaking task and will make it a less stressful experience? Nothing will be more off-putting and distracting for you and your audience than your having to constantly rearrange that 'smart' but uncomfortable clothing. I have been teaching for many years and always wear the same comfortable top that allows me to look smart but is not distracting and puts me off the task at hand. In relation to being in the moment (Chapter 3), it would be difficult to really be absorbed in your public speaking task if you are having to constantly adjust or are aware of an uncomfortable garment or blister-inducing footwear.

- *Physical fitness*
  - Public speaking can be quite tiring, especially if as discussed earlier (Chapter 3) you are quite passionate and enthusiastic about the topic. Mental energy, thinking on your feet, and responding to audience questions and input can leave you feeling quite drained. Apart from the more obvious outward appearance issues, being physically fit for the task is an aspect that is often neglected.
  - A recent survey (British active students survey report 2017/18) of 6,891 university students from 104 universities across the UK found that physical activity improved students' personal and mental wellbeing (see Further Resources). This survey showed clear evidence of the importance exercise and being active will have in both the nonverbal and verbal aspects of a public speaking performance.

Posture

If you were sitting in the audience and the speaker was slouched over with a poor posture, what would you think? Would it exude confidence and a feeling that this speaker is pleased to be there, enthusiastic and passionate about the topic they are about to present? Although the focus of this book has been on authenticity and being yourself, there are some occasions when nonverbally we need to make some changes. Posture is one of those aspects that can influence your fear of public speaking and how you are perceived by the audience.

An influential paper, whose author featured on the cover of *Time* magazine and a TED Talk viewed by millions, was published by Cuddy et al. (2012), based on research involving students at Harvard University's business school. They asked students to hold either a 'Low Power' (slouched) or 'High Power' (upright) posture for two minutes. Interestingly, the results indicated that those students with 'High Power' body language increased their testosterone levels and decreased cortisol (stress hormone), with a resultant increase in their assertiveness/confidence.

The key message from this research is that if you do not feel confident, act like it and your chances of success will greatly improve. This may be counterintuitive to authenticity, but important to mention and consider.

Interestingly, the above take on posture is that our body can influence our mind/fear of public speaking, whereas normally our mind influences how we act in certain circumstances. In the SUBH workshops, we discuss the influence of posture on our fear of public speaking, with most students feeling that there is an association between how we stand in front of an audience and our fear of public speaking. Regardless of whether we agree with the 'High Power' research, most students on the workshops state in the feedback that they are willing to try it out in their next public speaking task.

Practical steps to consider

- *Power pose*
    - Just before you are about to begin your presentation, stand upright (no slouching) and hold your arms out for two minutes; this would hopefully help you to reduce your stress levels and increase your confidence. I would not recommend you stroll into the presentation in this position but find a quiet place to do this just before you start. It may also help to focus your mind and be in the moment (Chapter 3) just before you start speaking.

- *Posture and breathing*
  - Try a slouched posture and see how this affects your breathing, as your lungs inflate and deflate with the associated ribcage movement. Many students will be aware of the impending physical and emotional changes that occur due to the 'fight and flight' response (Chapter 1) and may affect you as you are just about to speak. It is important to remember to breathe when speaking in public, and thus an upright posture is key to ensuring you are breathing adequately before and during your presentation.
- *Posture and voice*
  - Try slouching and speaking to a group of people as your voice is projected towards the floor. Do you think this is an effective method of projecting your voice and yourself? In many speaking situations you would not have the luxury of a microphone to project your voice, so that the audience are able to hear you fully. With an upright posture it is a lot easier to let your voice be heard without having to shout.

Student Voices

Strategies that are effective

'In a recent presentation I did a superman pose before my time to help me feel grounded and help regulate my breathing. During the presentation, I had an open posture and smiled to give myself confidence and engage the audience. I also did not hold my notes to allow me to express through my hands.'

Facial expression

Our facial expression is one of the more obvious aspects of nonverbal communication. Unless we are hiding under a desk or wearing a mask, the audience will have a view of our facial expression. If you are feeling petrified before and during public speaking, there is a strong possibility the audience will pick up on this. A well-worn and much used phrase, 'putting on a brave face', could literally be applied to our facial expression and what it may say about our underlying fear of public speaking.

The challenge all along with authenticity and nonverbal communication is the congruency between what we say and how we say it. If as discussed previously we are aiming to be authentic, not perfect and to have an element of authenticity (Chapter 3), then this could pose a challenge for us.

In my many years of public speaking, I have experienced occasions (especially when running workshops) when participants were paying to attend and I have had to contain and manage my fear. The audience were still seeing and hearing the real me, although I tried to give positive nonverbal signs, especially in my facial expression.

If we are trying to meet the needs of our audience, it is important to make that audience feel comfortable as this will enable them to respond to you more positively. There has been a lot written about the importance of making the audience feel comfortable as briefly mentioned in Chapter 3. Even if you are feeling nervous and slightly fearful in your presentation, try to smile and avoid a pained expression. This in turn will get the audience on side, have a positive effect on your public speaking fear and make the experience more positive.

We have focused on your facial expression up to now, but what about those of the audience? How many times have you looked out at a presentation only to be greeted by a sea of serious-looking faces, interspersed with the odd nodding head? This is one point that really strikes a chord with students on our SUBH workshops, as it is so easy to misinterpret the nonverbal facial expressions of an audience and thereby increase our fear. As previously discussed (Chapter 1), external fear generated by an audience is one of the main categories of fear that students experience in public speaking (LeFebvre et al., 2018). Try the individual activity below to help you understand an audience's reactions as expressed by their facial expression; this will help you manage your fear and understand those reactions a bit more.

Individual Activity

> When you last spoke in public, were all the audience smiling approvingly at you or did the majority have serious expressions?
>
> What do you think those expressions meant – were they positive or negative?

It may surprise you, but in my experience and as discussed in the SUBH workshops, those serious-looking faces are often listening faces: people are listening intently and concentrating on what you are saying. In my experience, this misinterpretation of audience facial expressions is the source of a lot of fear on behalf of students and those in public speaking. It is, however, easier to tell when the audience are falling asleep, bored, lacking concentration or their minds are somewhere else!

Next time you are speaking in public, give yourself credit and a pat on the back as there is a strong possibility the audience are listening intently and enjoying your talk.

Having said the above about audience facial expressions, we can sometimes get it wrong! I recently gave a talk to a group of philosophy students and totally misread their body language including facial expressions. Half way through the talk on fear of public speaking, I felt uncomfortable and slightly anxious as I felt they were not really interested and what I was saying was obvious. At the end of the talk, I was quite startled and pleasantly surprised when the finish was greeted by a round of applause.

Eye communication

There is a fair amount of evidence on the use and importance of eye contact in everyday communication. In public speaking this is an important skill that is often neglected when we are feeling fearful and would rather be anywhere else but in front of an audience. I can recall many occasions when students were so nervous that they spent all their time fixing their gaze on the PC screen in front of them or were head down reading their presentation script. In fact, even those students who appeared confident about public speaking did not look at the audience enough.

The vulnerability that we feel when standing up and speaking in public sometimes makes it difficult to make eye contact. As previously discussed (Chapter 1) students often felt judged and did not like the audience`s eyes on them as they stood out front. Therefore, it is understandable that making eye contact with the audience could be challenging for some students. Related to the vulnerability issue is that of being in the moment when speaking in public and being fully engaged; this can be achieved by trying to maintain eye contact with the audience.

It is not only students who get eye communication wrong in public speaking. I remember on one occasion when we were recruiting for a new member of staff at the university. One of the candidates caught my eye (excuse the pun) for the wrong reasons, as he seemed more preoccupied with what was going on outside the window than with what was happening inside the seminar room. In a strange way this made me feel unsettled as it seemed to depersonalise the speaking situation, and as an audience member I felt taken for granted!

Eye contact is our nonverbal way of connecting with the audience, and as mentioned before, getting them on side. To be truly conversational with your audience (Chapter 4) you need to make eye contact with them. If you don't connect with them, this will ensure they lose interest and get bored – and their reaction will only increase your fear.

> ## Student Voices
> ### Difficulty of making eye contact
> *'Just reading from notes and not making eye contact, this was the only way I could actually do one [presentation] in the first place.'*
>
> *'Not looking at the audience, focusing on a point behind them.'*

Practical steps to consider

- *Scan your gaze*
    - Next time you are giving a presentation try to start looking at the audience. Some people will stare straight ahead at the mass of people thinking that this is eye communication. In a recent SUBH workshop, a few of the participants were either too nervous to make eye contact or thought that gazing just above the audience's heads was OK.
    - As in a conversation, maintain eye contact but only intermittently with members of the audience as you scan your gaze around the room. Various timescales have been proposed ranging from 3 to 5 seconds for you to hold your eye contact with an individual member of the audience. Whatever feels right for you and the person you are looking at would be my advice. Importantly, make sure your gaze is not too long as this may become uncomfortable for the particular audience member concerned. Also, how you look around the room is down to personal choice, although try to ensure you distribute your gaze equally around the room and don't concentrate on one corner of the audience. A useful technique would be to scan from left to right or right to left in a methodical way.
- *Avoid the stare*
    - In scanning your gaze around the room, it is easy to settle on a friendly face for longer than is comfortable. I remember

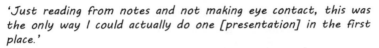

once staring a little bit too long at a student who turned to her friend and commented on this sustained eye contact. I felt terrible about this and quite embarrassed afterwards. In the same way we conversationally maintain eye contact, we will usually know or get signals when we have overstayed our welcome!

- *Do not read too much into the audience reaction*
  - While looking around the room and making eye contact, it is easy as discussed previously to get the wrong message. That listening face may appear to you as severe and disapproving, when in fact the person is engrossed in what you have to say. Just remember that you are maintaining eye contact with audience members to ensure you connect with them and appreciate their listening to you. Regardless of what you think their reaction is nonverbally, they will thank you afterwards for making the effort to communicate.

Movement and gestures

To be an authentic public speaker you do not need to be rooted to the spot or attached to a podium or microphone stand. In some speaking situations the PC and IT equipment will be situated where we tend to stand for ease of access. I forget the amount of times I have seen a student attach themself to the podium, gripping on for dear life as they give their presentation. This static posture is certainly no way to reduce or manage a fear of public speaking.

I have found that moving around is a great way to reduce my stress and keep me in the moment when public speaking. If you observe many of the speakers in TED Talks they are not hidden behind a podium or microphone stand but are out in front talking to the audience. Initially this may seem daunting, but in many ways it is liberating and allows you to fully connect with your audience. How can you demonstrate your nonverbal skills as discussed in this chapter and fully meet the needs of an audience if you are hiding behind a podium?

Apart from movement another key nonverbal form of communication is the use of hand gestures. Gestures reinforce an argument, show passion, give confidence to an audience, communicate thoughts effortlessly and enhance authenticity (McNeill, 2008). In our SUBH workshops, many students have mentioned that they have often been advised to use fewer gestures in their presentations. This can lead to a rigid, robotic and far from authentic style of public speaking. This is not straightforward advice, as many people find their ability to communicate is closely linked to hand gestures. It is very difficult to be passionate and enthusiastic if your hands are held tightly together, and you feel compelled to keep your gestures to a minimum, when that is counterintuitive. Quite a few students have mentioned that culturally it is quite normal for them to use hand gestures all the time in their daily conversation.

The other argument used is that the audience will find this distracting and this then reduces your overall impact. Granted, it may be a bit distracting at times, but if it enables you to feel less nervous and present confidently, then I would strongly encourage it.

One of the exercises we do in the SUBJH workshops that many students find useful is to pair up and try different hand gesture positions when talking to each other. I would highly recommend the following individual activity that you could try out in various public speaking situations.

Individual Activity

How does it feel when you try one of the following when speaking in public, and which single or combination relating to hand gestures do you feel most comfortable doing? Underline the hand gesture behaviour that appeals to you most:

- Hands by your side/in pockets
- Use gestures all the time
- Use gestures sparingly at key moments/ emphasise a point

- Gestures below belly button/waist
- Gestures above waist (within power sphere)

According to McNeill (2008), the power sphere is when our hand gestures are between our belly button and ears.

Interestingly, most participants on the SUBH workshops found using gestures sparingly and within the 'power sphere' the most natural form of gesturing while speaking. There were a small minority who found using gestures all the time their preferred option.

Student Voice

Benefits of nonverbal techniques

'Nonverbal techniques are factors that I now consider more when presenting, for example my posture and eye contact with the audience. Even though I dislike standing in front of an audience, it does help my delivery compared to sitting. Movement is something I struggle with, but I do find gestures beneficial. I feel if I presented regularly, movement and facial expressions are something that I would practise using. I've also discovered that positive affirmations prior to presenting is very beneficial.'

Putting it all together

'The workshop inspired a different approach to delivering presentations on placement, considering nonverbal communication techniques to interact with the audience such as facial expressions, eye contact and using simple gestures to command the space. This is combined with ensuring I understand the topic and including telling a story. I've felt more confident to use pictures in slides, sometimes with just a few words, helping to illustrate ideas and express authenticity.'

Chapter summary

Hopefully as you read through this chapter, you recognised the importance of nonverbal communication and how it can help you become a more authentic and less fearful public speaker. This chapter should enable you to become more authentic by ensuring you are aware of your nonverbal behaviour and has covered the following aspects, namely appearance, posture, facial expression, eye communication, and movement and gestures. As previously discussed, the key is to ensure that your nonverbal communication is in harmony and matches up with what you are saying. This is important as it will decrease your authenticity and be noticed by the audience. Finally, please do not forget to complete the reflective space at the end of this chapter that will be beneficial in you using and being aware of the importance of nonverbal communication in public speaking.

Reflective Space

Using this reflective space will give you an opportunity to review and consolidate what has been covered in this chapter. This might be something that you have not done much of, but in my experience and those of students in the SUBH workshops, it has proved really helpful.

Reflect on what could you take home from this chapter in respect of nonverbal communication. Specifically:

Which of the following in the table do you think you are not really using in public speaking?

How could each of the five forms of nonverbal communication be used more effectively?

Table 6.1

	Not using in public speaking (tick below)	**More effective use (describe below)**
Appearance		
Posture		
Facial expression		
Eye contact		
Movement and gesture		

7

Practice and Preparation

OVERVIEW

This chapter will focus on the importance of practice and preparation for public speaking. It is claimed that some people are either naturally good at public speaking or they are not. Regardless of this innate ability, effective practice and preparation are key for the confident student and even more so if they have a fear of public speaking. Most of the chapter will focus on ways to practise that will help you manage your fear and in turn make you a more authentic public speaker. Note that this is not an overnight process, and becoming more confident in public speaking may take a while as you will need to discover which approach is the most effective for you.

Individual Activity

When sitting at home watching TV, and a footballer dribbles around his opponent with the ball attached to his feet or a tennis player smashes the ball over the net, consider how they made this look easy. Was it justtheir natural innate skill that achieved this or hours of practice? Or maybe a bit of both?! Try to relate this to your fear and ability in relation to public speaking.

Consider the following statements and circle yes/no as appropriate:

- 'My fear increases and I am not as effective if I am not well prepared and have fully practised for my presentation.' (yes/no)
- 'My fear decreases and I am effective if I am well prepared and have fully practised for my presentation.' (yes/no)

Further to the individual activity above, many students who have a fear or find public speaking difficult are often in one of two camps or both, namely:

- 'I have a fear of public speaking and do not fully appreciate the importance of practice.'
- 'I have a fear of fear of public speaking, appreciate the importance of practice, but am not sure how to do it effectively.'

You might be in the first, second or both camps in relation to public speaking and practice. In respect of the above example of the sports person excelling at their sport, they may have been a natural but without the practice and preparation they would not have reached their level of skill. Have a quick think about anything you have really excelled at – I would be surprised if this did not take a fair amount of time and effective practice to get there!

In our SUBH workshops, many of the students do not fully realise the importance of practice and preparation in making them effective at public speaking. The example that I give, and one that has been well publicised, is Steve Jobs, the former CEO of Apple. According to Gallo (2014), Steve Jobs was initially very nervous about public speaking early on in his career, but over the years due to his reputation for practising for hours for a presentation, he made his public speaking look effortless. Therefore, apart from the authenticity approach to public speaking, the other key take-home message for all of us is practice. Further to this is practising effectively to ensure we are well prepared and in turn less fearful of our public speaking task. Significantly, although the time spent here is important, how we practise and the quality of that practice are often even more essential. Some of the key factors in student learning, according to Race (2015), that we can apply to practising public speaking include '*doing*' and '*verbalising*'. Both factors relate to the experience of practising the presentation and saying it out loud which we will cover in this chapter.

Individual Activity

Write down in this box any aspects, fears and issues related to your public speaking that you need to practise and improve.

Your own responses in the individual activity above will hopefully be the impetus and motivation for you to want to improve and spend time in learning and practising your public speaking.

Right, let's get to work and review a few practice ideas.

Refresh your memory

Before we start concentrating on the practice aspect of public speaking, please have a look at Figure 7.1 on p. 104, which is an overview of the authentic approach and all the related strategies we have covered so far. While reviewing the varying ideas and approaches to practising your public speaking skills, it would be a good idea to refresh your memory by referring to Figure 7.1 or the related chapters. All the material and strategies we have been through are fundamental to managing your fear and should be incorporated in your practice and preparation. Also, ensure that you go through 'The Basics: A Chronological Checklist' (Chapter 5) to ensure those basics are completed before, during and after your presentation. They are not practice focused but essential to your presentation and should not be excluded.

Breathing exercise

As mentioned earlier in this study guide, breathing and our awareness of it is essential in public speaking to increase your confidence and control your fear. Further to the discussion on 'fight or flight' (Chapter 1) and rapid shallow chest breathing in Chapter 4, we will now look at a breathing exercise that focuses on the more effective deep abdominal breathing (diaphragmatic breathing). This method of breathing is also used by actors and singers to project their voice, which adds to the benefit of practising and using this technique in public speaking. With practice, this type of breathing will become easier and more automatic when standing up to speak.

Relaxed deep (diaphragmatic) breathing

Relaxed deep breathing involves use of the dome-shaped diaphragm muscle which separates our chest (thorax) and abdomen. Diaphragmatic breathing is an efficient and relaxed way of getting enough air into your lungs and slowing down your breathing. Put

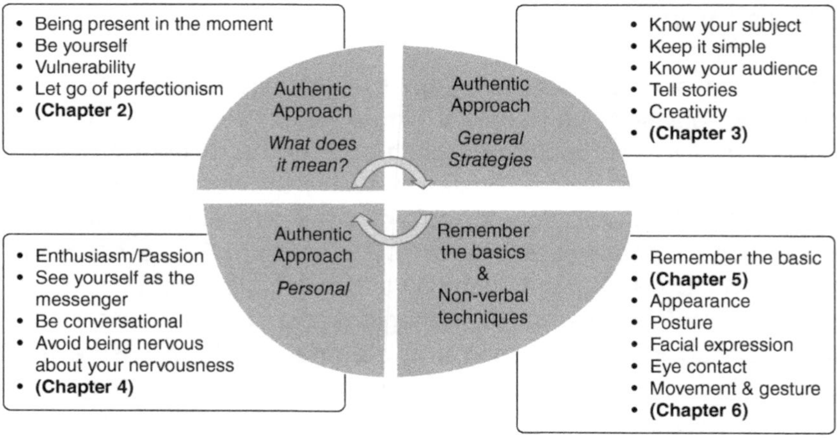

Figure 7.1 An overview of the authentic approach with related strategies covered in this study guide

simply, when we *breathe in* the diaphragm contracts and our stomach pushes out, and when we *breathe out* the diaphragm relaxes and our stomach flattens. You will feel the stomach movement under your hands in the breathing exercise below. I will not go into further detail on the exact mechanics of respiration and diaphragmatic breathing as there is a lot of information on this subject that is easy to access. I would advise you to try the following exercise.

This relaxed deep-breathing exercise and variations of it are well known and commonly described in the literature in relation to breathing and stress:

1. This exercise can be done standing up, lying or sitting down. Ensure you are not slouched, with your head or chest forward.
2. Your eyes can be open or closed.
3. First just concentrate on your breathing and note how fast or slow it is, and whether you are breathing mainly from your chest or using your diaphragm effectively (points 4 to 6 will confirm this).
4. Place one hand on your chest and the other on your upper stomach just below your ribs.

5. Now breathe in slowly through your nose and you should feel your hand being pushed out on your stomach, while there is minimal chest movement. You could count to 3 or 4 while you breathe in.
6. Then slowly breathe out through your mouth and feel your stomach flatten. You could count to 3 or 4 while you breathe out.
7. Try this diaphragmatic breathing at least two or three times and on at least a daily basis until it becomes automatic and requires minimal thought.
8. Further to this breathing exercise, practise speaking or saying a word as you breathe out and your stomach flattens. This will ensure the correct timing of speaking and breathing, and will increase the volume and projection of your voice. This is one of the ways a singer or actor can ensure the audience at the back of the hall can hear them speaking or singing.

Using relaxed deep (diaphragmatic) breathing in your public speaking

- Remember to use this breathing technique when you are aware of your nervousness just prior to speaking, and that nervousness is a normal response to public speaking (Chapter 4).
- If during the talk you suddenly become consumed with nerves, pause, take a few deep breaths (diagrammatic breathing) and then continue.

Practise out loud and include self-assessment

If you have spent hours preparing your PowerPoint (or any other visual slides) (see Chapter 5 for ideas on presenting visual slides) and have these printed out in a handout, you have not fully completed the preparation for your presentation. Many students I come across unfortunately make this mistake, and then find this out the hard way when standing in front of an audience.

Although this putting together of PowerPoint slides may have taken you many hours, particularly if you avoided copious amounts of text and included diagrams, graphics and referenced material, you will have only taken the first step!

Hopefully you followed the module presentation guidelines, know how long your presentation should be timewise, included only relevant material, showed your knowledge and understanding of the subject, and kept it simple as described in previous strategies (Chapter 3). As your public speaking presentation involves talking and presenting to an audience I would advise the following:

1. *Initially, say your speech/presentation* ***to yourself*** *out loud at the pace and volume you plan to present on the day.* You could either use cue cards with the main points or put down key points next to each of the slides on your handout. Some people avoid too much text on their slides and just use graphics with key words or terms. Project the presentation via your laptop and go through each slide as if you were giving a presentation. Even better, if possible try and practise your presentation out loud in the same room in the university campus where you will be presenting. If possible stand at the podium or in the floor space and use the same IT equipment you will use on the day. If this is not possible any room at home where you can talk out loud without disturbance will do.
   - During your rehearsal try using some visualisation involving you giving your presentation; this will make your practice more real and applicable to your planned presentation (see the section on pp. 117–8: Putting visualisation into practice). After your practice presentation, try the self-assessment below in the individual activity section to see how you did and where you could improve. This will ensure that your practice and rehearsal time is effective and not wasted. Completing the self-assessment will also enable you to focus on those areas of your presentation that need more attention.

Individual Activity

How do you think you did?

Circle the applicable Yes/No/Nearly there for each question:

1. Did you follow the presentation guidelines and keep to the allotted time?

   Yes/No/Nearly there

2. Did you avoid being nervous about your nervousness?

   Yes/No/Nearly there

3. Were you authentic (see Chapter 2)?

   Yes/No/Nearly there

4. Did you focus on the message and communication and not just your performance?

   Yes/No/Nearly there

5. Were you enthusiastic and passionate?

   Yes/No/Nearly there

6. Did you know your subject and keep it simple?

   Yes/No/Nearly there

7. Were the visual slides interesting (graphics, diagrams) and not text dominant?

   Yes/No/Nearly there

8. Did you say and not entirely read your presentation?

   Yes/No/Nearly there

9. Were you aware of your facial expression, posture and eye contact (imaginary audience)?

   Yes/No/Nearly there

10. Was there a match (congruency) between your verbal and nonverbal behaviour?

    Yes/No/Nearly there

Score yourself out of 10 for above questions ………/10

Score yourself out of 10 for your fear/nervousness. ………/10

Total score………/10

2. *Now, say your speech/presentation out loud to a friend or friends (family members will do) at the pace and volume you plan to present on the day.* This is when it may be a bit more difficult, but you are now starting to make your practice or preparation fit for purpose. Years ago I used to run marathons, and part of the training involved getting used to being on your feet for hours and replicating what running 26 miles would be like. The same goes for public speaking. Unless you plan to read your presentation, just preparing PowerPoint slides will result in you reading and not really presenting. Remember to stick to your allocated time and allow for a few extra minutes at the end as you will most probably speak more quickly on the day. As mentioned above, during your rehearsal try using some visualisation involving you giving your presentation; this will make your practice more real and applicable to your planned presentation (see section on pp. 117–8: Putting visualisation into practice).
   - As previously, try and complete the self-assessment below which will be very beneficial in monitoring your practice progression.

Individual Activity

How do you think you did?

Circle the applicable Yes/No/Nearly there for each question:

1. Did you follow the presentation guidelines and keep to the allotted time?

   Yes/No/Nearly there

2. Did you avoid being nervous about your nervousness?

   Yes/No/Nearly there

3. Were you authentic (see Chapter 2)?

   Yes/No/Nearly there

4. Did you focus on the message and communication and not just your performance?

   Yes/No/Nearly there

5. Were you enthusiastic and passionate?

   Yes/No/Nearly there

6. Did you know your subject and keep it simple?

   Yes/No/Nearly there

7. Were the visual slides interesting (graphics, diagrams) and not text dominant?

   Yes/No/Nearly there

8. Did you say and not entirely read your presentation?

   Yes/No/Nearly there

9. Were you aware of your facial expression, posture and eye contact?

   Yes/No/Nearly there

10. Was there a match (congruency) between your verbal and nonverbal behaviour?

    Yes/No/Nearly there

Score yourself out of 10 for above questions. /10

Score yourself out of 10 for your fear/nervousness. /10

Total score /10

You should now notice a difference in the scoring between doing your practice run to yourself and to a person or group of people. I would advise you to practise and rehearse to a point where you score highly (in both rehearsal scenarios, i.e. with and without an audience). You should reach a point where you are not having to think too much about your presentation and it starts to look easy and relaxed! As mentioned above, this may take a while and a few practice runs to achieve.

Student Voice

Practising my presentation

'Before I give a presentation, the thing that makes me feel the most prepared and relaxed is having the opportunity to practise. As I am preparing each slide for the presentation I start thinking about what I will say and make a note of this as I go along. Doing this helps me to feel prepared and ensures I am including the relevant information. Then, I spend time practising the presentation saying it out loud to myself and use a timer to help me keep within the set time for the presentation. When I am practising I find it helpful to stand up as I would during the presentation. This helps me to feel confident, get familiar with my posture and reduce my reliance on reading from the slides. I also practise my presentation in front of friends and family, who often give feedback which is helpful.'

Recording, feedback and reflection

Recording

Further to self-assessment, many people will record or video themselves practising their presentation. Personally, I have always avoided doing this as I do not like to see or hear myself speak. We have lecture capture software at my university where all our lectures are recorded for students. This lecture capture can include a video and/or voice recording of the lecture. In my few years of using lecture capture I ensure the video is turned off so that only my voice is captured, and I do not listen to a recording of the lecture. Technically, I am missing a great opportunity to review my presentation and make changes accordingly. You may be OK with hearing your voice and seeing yourself on video. If you are, I would recommend this approach and ask one of your family or friends to video your practice presentation or record yourself speaking on your phone. This would be useful and assist in your self-assessment as described above.

Feedback

Further to practising in front of people, try and get them to give you some feedback. Feedback is an important tool and factor in improving and getting to grips with public speaking, and according to Race (2015) is one of the key factors in successful learning at university. As a university student, regardless of your level of study, you should hopefully have received some sort of feedback on written coursework, presentations, exams and other forms of assessment. The quality of feedback varies but is invaluable in your learning and improving your skill in a specific task. If you are assessed in public speaking/presentations, please ensure you read your written feedback and if possible arrange to speak to your examiner to gain further input on what went well and could be improved. Many students in all forms of assessment will often just look at the overall grade and not read the feedback.

In my experience, students with lower (than they expected) grades tend to focus or seek verbal feedback as to why they received the grades they did. I would hope that students who gained a high grade also took note of all their feedback to get an even higher grade in the future! On another note, be careful not to focus too highly on your grades, as it is what you learn, and the skills you acquire at university, that will be applied in your future life and employment, not grades!

Further to your self-assessment, after rehearsing your presentation out loud first to yourself and then to a small audience, it is important you receive feedback from a person or people you trust. Recently my daughter had a presentation to give on her university programme. Overall she is not fearful of public speaking, but found the opportunity to give her presentation to my wife and I (at least three times) and receive feedback was a key factor in ensuring a successful outcome for her assessed presentation. Giving feedback can be difficult at times, but it is important that the person giving it focuses on the positive and negative aspects and gives you constructive feedback. The ten questions used in the individual activity self-assessment could be used by the audience member giving you feedback. Receiving feedback can also be challenging, so ensure that the person giving it is someone you trust and respect. Once you have received that feedback, reflect on it and try to discuss together the ways you can improve.

Reflection

Without reflection it is difficult to consolidate on your learning and move forward in relation to reducing your fear and improving your public speaking. As you will have noticed, we have reflective spaces at the end of each chapter in this book which I would strongly encourage you to use. In the literature there are a number of models for reflection that can assist you in reflecting on a task. The example included here is one for self-reflection called a SWOT analysis: it is used by students and anyone who wants to reflect on their **S**trengths, **W**eaknesses, **O**pportunities and **T**hreats in relation to a task, performance or situation. Many of our physiotherapy students, for example, complete a SWOT analysis at the beginning and end of their clinical placements. When discussing the SWOT analysis with them, it is interesting how many have a list of weaknesses and only one or two strengths. It is important to be as honest as possible in relation to your strengths and weakness that are internal to you, and to also give some thought to the opportunities and threats that are external. The key is to realise that there is a relationship between these four factors/variables; have you any thoughts on what this relationship could be?

Below is an example of a SWOT analysis I would have done a few years ago in relation to my public speaking, i.e. giving a lecture. This was a time when I struggled giving lectures more than I do now, and focused too much on my stammer and how I came across to the audience.

Table 7.1 Personal SWOT analysis in respect of author giving lectures

Strengths Approachable Enthusiastic Knowledgeable Graphic text-free visual slides Evidence-based presentation (Turning point: Self-disclosure Attitude change)	**Weaknesses** Fluency, problem saying certain words Focus on how not what I say Style over substance Nervous about my communication skills Speaking too fast
Opportunities PG Cert HE when first employed Attended one presentation workshop Support from colleagues Module feedback from students	**Threats** Students not interested Students late for lecture Low attendance levels Use of mobile phone Lecture theatre too narrow and not suitable for learning IT playing up

Looking at the above SWOT analysis there are some clear and identifiable issues in relation to my public speaking. The *strengths* could be used to tackle the *threats* and the *weakness* either offset by the *strengths* or reduced by the *opportunities*. I did not feel the opportunities or support were very effective while I was struggling with some of my public speaking issues, and to be honest I felt quite alone. For me the key turning point was when I started using self-disclosure before lectures (only once per cohort of students, then not for subsequent lectures) about my stammer. Some of the initial looks on students' faces were interesting, but the overall response was always very positive. This result from self-disclosure meant that I could now focus on what I was saying instead of that dread of stammering and how I was presenting. This resulted in a more authentic approach and a complete change of attitude. As per the SWOT analysis, the outcome was more engaged students and lectures, and a possible increase in attendance and interest by students. Importantly, however hard I tried to sort out the internal weaknesses there were some external threats that were beyond my control, i.e. students arriving late for lectures, low attendance levels, use of mobile phones, and a lecture theatre that was too narrow and not suitable for learning.

Although the strengths may counteract the threats, there will be times when it may be impossible to overcome all the threats. Importantly, using a SWOT analysis in your reflection will lead to a greater all-round understanding of the internal and external factors impacting on your public speaking. This in turn will show you which areas to focus on and what may be beyond your control. Ultimately, you may also be kinder to yourself when some of your public speaking efforts do not go as well as planned.

Right, I have shared my SWOT analysis with you, so in the individual activity below try to do a SWOT analysis for yourself. Remember, this will not only help you understand more about your public speaking, it will also guide you on which areas to focus on in your practice and preparation. Spending time on reflection now will pay dividends in your public speaking future.

Individual Activity

Try and do a SWOT analysis below and include some strengths and not too many weaknesses. If you can discuss your SWOT analysis with someone this may prove helpful to you, although it's not essential. Once completed, focus on all the aspects to guide you in your practice and show where there is room for improvement.

Table 7.2 SWOT analysis

Strengths	Weaknesses

Opportunities	Threats

Using visualisation in your public speaking practice

In Chapter 1, I briefly mentioned and discussed social anxiety disorder (SAD) and that this or other mental health issues may be the reason for your fear or public speaking anxiety. I therefore recommended that some students may need further intensive psychological therapy (CBT, counselling, etc.) that is beyond the scope of the SUBH workshops and my expertise. In the same light, although this book may be of some use to you, it may be limited in helping you fully manage or overcome your fear of public speaking. Although I am not a psychologist, we do briefly cover visualisation techniques in our SUBH workshops which the students do find useful. The section below will briefly incorporate some CBT psychological therapies, specifically visualisation/mental imagery, that are widely used in improving sport performance and applicable to managing fear or improving public speaking.

The above practice ideas in this chapter have included rehearsal and physically saying your presentation out loud, and incorporating the use of feedback and self-reflection (SWOT analysis). In the above section I mentioned using visualisation or mental imagery to ensure your practice is more real and applicable to your planned presentation. An important take-home message is that, although there is evidence for the use of visualisation techniques for fear of public speaking, Ayres and Ayres (1994) point out that inadequate preparation is an important but largely undocumented source of speech anxiety. Although this is an earlier statement, the evidence provided from students attending our SUBH workshops, and those we assess in presentations, supports the view that inadequate practice and preparation is a key factor in public speaking fear.

Visualisation/mental imagery

Research studies on visualisation have found that it is effective in reducing public speaking anxiety/fear (comprehension apprehension) in university students. Further research on communication studies students has indicated that performance visualisation techniques could also be used to enhance the performance aspects of public speaking and decrease speech anxiety.

Below are some important points and definitions related to visualisation, with the relevant research mentioned, in case you wanted to do some further reading:

- *Visualisation* (Ayres and Hopf, 1985, 1989) is effective in reducing student fear of public speaking and uses a script to take a person through the day on which they are speaking/presenting, with an emphasis on imagining a positive outcome. Public speaking anxiety (particularly moderate or high public speaking anxiety) was lower in those university students who used visualisation compared to those who did not and if used more than once.
- *Performance visualisation* (Ayres and Ayres, 1994; Ayres and Ayres Sonandre, 2003) is effective in reducing student fear of public speaking and may enhance the public speaking performance. Performance visualisation is closely linked to a method used to improve athletes' performance. An example used by the above researchers is of a tennis player who does not just imagine herself playing well, but also watches a video of a tennis player who serves perfectly and then aims to re-create an image of herself executing the same perfect serve. Performance visualisation would use the same approach for public speaking fear and to enhance public speaking. Performance visualisation of a student speaker is more effective in reducing public speaking anxiety for students than performance visualisation featuring just a great speaker. Targeting specific behaviours rather than exposing people to an entire speech might enhance the effectiveness of performance visualisation. A limitation of performance visualisation is that

people with reduced image ability would gain less benefit than those who see images more vividly.

Putting visualisation into practice

In some of the previous research above a step-by-step script was used for the student in visualising from the time they woke up in the morning to giving their presentation. Apart from using the visualisation script below, remember to visualise the presentation process positively and do it at least a few times prior to the day for best results.

Below is a modified step-by-step visualisation script for you that is closely aligned with material presented in this book. The following steps in chronological order might help you positively visualise your next presentation. Remember to incorporate the material we have covered in this book as part of your visualisation (see Figure 7.1 for an overview) and pointers with a (*) below:

1. *Imagine* yourself getting up in the morning, ready for your presentation having prepared adequately and really knowing your topic (*see Practice and Preparation, Chapter 7).
2. *Imagine* yourself adequately prepared, wearing the right comfortable clothing, having prepared your visual slides and handouts, and getting to the venue in plenty of time and setting up the IT equipment (*see Basics, Chapter 5).
3. *Imagine* your opening lines and nonverbal behaviour (*fill in the nonverbal behaviour that appeals to you and that we covered in Chapter 6) as you positively make eye contact with the audience; remember to breathe.
4. *Imagine* being an authentic, enthusiastic speaker, one who is not perfect but knows their subject and is a messenger meeting the needs of the audience (*fill in the authenticity strategies we covered in Chapters 3 and 4).
5. *Imagine* your authentic conversational approach is going down well with the audience who appear interested in what you have to say.
6. *Imagine* you conclude and give a good overview at the end of your presentation and you can answer the audience questions effectively.

7. *Imagine* your feelings of satisfaction at overcoming a fear, or if not fearful just being an effective communicator and giving a great presentation/speech.

Putting performance visualisation into practice

Performance visualisation uses imagery as described above, but is different from visualisation in that a student would watch a video of a proficient speaker, make a mental movie and then replace the speaker on the video with a clear image of themself as the speaker. This approach is also effective for a student with or without a fear of public speaking. Remember that for both visualisation approaches, although the research evidence as described above has found they are effective in public speaking fear, not all people are effective in image ability which may reduce visualisation effectiveness.

Try and find a video of a student (evidence supports this as opposed to any great speaker) or someone you admire who you think has the presentation style that you aspire towards. You could video a fellow student (with their permission), or view some of the many great videos on TED Talks. Below are some steps you could follow in performance visualisation:

- Once the video is up you would decide if you want to re-create an image of yourself giving all the presentation/speech in their style or just using certain aspects. How the speaker interacts with the audience, their nonverbal behaviour, opening or closing could all be areas to focus on.
- You may need to replay, rewind or forward certain parts of the video numerous times to get a clear mental picture in your mind.
- You would then make a mental movie and replace the speaker on the video with a clear image of yourself as the speaker.
- As with visualisation you may need a few performance visualisation runs to gain any benefits from this approach.

Further to the survey we conducted of student fears of public speaking (Grieve et al., 2019), one of the six main themes that emerged in relation to the open question 'What strategies have you used to reduce your fear of public speaking (including presentations)?' was that of '*Practising and preparation*'. This is very encouraging and relevant as it confirms that, although there may be issues in respect of how to practise, the students we surveyed in the majority realise the importance of practising public speaking. Many of the practice techniques are described in this chapter. Below are some of the student voices (comments/quotes) in relation to a fear of public speaking and university experience that you may find you can identify with as a student getting to grips with public speaking. Even as an experienced university lecturer, I can identify with many of these student voices.

Student Voices

Practising and preparation

'Talking presentation through out loud.'

'Breathing exercises beforehand.'

'Breathing slowly.'

'Practise before giving the presentation, e.g. talking to the cats!'

'Reading slides to myself.'

'Recording a practice presentation to view myself.'

'Recording notes on my phone.'

'Practise to peers.'

'Present the presentation to a small selection of people, whom I find intimidating, to rehearse the presentation and get ready for when it comes to presenting the presentation in front of a large group of highly knowledgeable experts and professionals.'

'Rehearsing the presentation beforehand.'

Chapter summary

This comprehensive chapter should give you the information and skills to ensure your public speaking practice and preparation are worthwhile and effective. We have reviewed practical ways to practise out loud that incorporate feedback, reflection and self-assessment. Further ideas on visualisation are also presented. Many public speaking commentators and writers advocate hours of practice to manage public speaking fear and become an effective speaker. This may be true, but what is key here is practice quality, not quantity, and ensuring it is fit for purpose! The student voices presented in this chapter on practising may give you some food for thought and encouragement in your preparation for public speaking. Finally, please do complete the reflective space as this will reinforce what has been covered in this chapter.

Reflective Space

Using this reflective space will give you an opportunity to review and consolidate what has been covered in this chapter. This might be something you have not done much of, but in my experience and those of students in the SUBH workshops, it has proved really helpful.

What could you take home from this chapter in respect of how to practise effectively for public speaking?

Are there any student voices at the end of this chapter that you can identify with and learn lessons from?

8

The Benefits of Standing Up and Being Heard

OVERVIEW

This chapter will reinforce the fact that public speaking does not just focus on presentations but is a transferable skill for use throughout your university career. How you approach, view and are involved in public speaking may affect your student experience, employability and beyond. In focusing on the negative aspects of public speaking, we often forget about the importance of this transferable life skill, and hence this brief chapter will mainly focus on the positives in relation to public speaking. Initially we will briefly review how a fear of public speaking may affect your university experience. The chapter will look at the benefits of public speaking in relation to the many teaching and learning activities from assessed presentations to extra-curricular activities that you may be involved in.

As discussed previously (Chapter 1), one of the six themes that emerged from a qualitative survey (Grieve et al., 2019) we conducted was that a fear of public speaking had a '*Negative effect on university experience*' for most of the students who attended the SUBH workshops. I have included many of the comments/quotes previously, but in summary the main findings were that this fear of public speaking affected, the following: grades due to presentation ability, students put off modules with a presentation element, not asking questions to increase understanding and an anxiety/fear to speak in class. As you can see these are all important aspects of university involvement that are fundamental to your learning.

Before we review and discuss some of the benefits of public speaking, it would be a good idea for you to reflect on what you see as some of the main benefits of public speaking as a university student.

Individual Activity

Jot down here what you feel are the three key benefits of public speaking to you as a student. (You may wish to include a specific learning activity that involves public speaking.)

Previously, we briefly discussed the following range of university-based activities that may be affected by your fear of public speaking. This included but was not purely focused on presentations, namely:

- Presentations
- Seminars
- Lectures
- Practical exams
- Viva voce
- Extra-curricular activities
- Any others, please list below:
- ……………………………………..
- ………………………………………

Let's now focus on each of the above learning activities, and how the transferable skill of public speaking is fundamental to your successful involvement in each of these university activities and may be transferred for employability and later life.

Student Voice

Group presentation

'Today as part of one of my modules I had to take part in a group presentation. After taking your advice on board I felt the most confident I have ever been when presenting and noticed many of my usual worries and anxious signs weren't there/ weren't anywhere near as bad as usual.

I appreciate this was a group presentation rather than individual, but it has really helped. Others in my group even fed back how confident I came across (not knowing I had attended your course).

So, I just wanted to say thank you, the work you do is great and I'm even looking forward to doing the next presentation (never thought I'd say that!).'

Presentations

As a student many of the modules that make up your programme of study are assessed by a presentation, with the grades affecting your overall degree classification. Apart from module presentation assessments, presentation skills are essential for the some of the following:

- *Research* – In our final-year undergraduate research module we have a research conference where we ask students to give a platform or poster presentation. The ability to present and disseminate research is fundamental in this instance. Importantly, this skill is key if you plan to pursue a research-based career or will be conducting research that you would want to present at a conference. Leading research teams or speaking to potential researchers and/or groups of participants also requires presentation skills. If you apply for ethical approval for a research project, you may need to present or respond to questions from an ethics board and perhaps present your proposed research project.
- *Employability* – Apart from module presentations, many jobs require and advocate public speaking skills. From advertising to law and many spheres of business, you will need to be able to pitch or present an idea and be comfortable speaking in public. Many of our students involved

in health-related occupations need to be able to present an overview of a treatment plan or patient progress as part of a multidisciplinary team. It could be argued that some people do not apply for certain positions or that their job promotion may be limited because of presentation fear.

- As mentioned previously I had a fear of public speaking that has improved over time, mainly due to using the authenticity approach as advocated in this book. Interestingly, only recently I have come across both inexperienced and highly experienced university lecturers who have a fear of public speaking, but are aware of this and have used their nervous energy and spent time practising and preparing to improve their public speaking. The result has often been positive feedback from students in response to teaching on their respective modules.
- *Life skills* – Given that a fear of public speaking, and particularly presentations, affects so many people and not just students, the benefits of managing this are numerous. Apart from increasing employment skills, a sense of self-satisfaction and confidence would be high on the list. Importantly, overcoming or mastering something you find difficult would certainly increase your self-confidence, which would also positively increase your interpersonal and communication life skills in general. Importantly, public speaking is a transferable skill that is essential for enabling you to demonstrate your knowledge and expertise to employers and clients alike.

Seminars

Due to large cohort sizes many university programmes use seminars as an opportunity for students to learn in smaller groups. In seminars you would often be asked to read a paper or complete a task beforehand and then discuss the findings with other students. Public speaking skills are needed as you discuss concepts and ideas amongst a few student colleagues or across the whole seminar group. Further to discussing and sharing ideas, asking questions is a fundamental skill for increasing your learning. Some students do not use the opportunity to increase their learning by asking questions due to a public speaking fear. It is necessary to realise here that often when you ask a question many of your fellow students would have a similar question in mind.

Employability and life skills

Apart from university-based learning, being able to discuss concepts, share ideas and ask questions is a key skill suited for many areas of employment. Apart from employment these skills are essential for daily life, from enquiries related to purchasing products, or discussing health issues with a doctor, to asking about ingredients in a menu when ordering food.

Lectures

Many lecture halls are crammed with students, sometimes in the hundreds. When I give a lecture, the number of students who ask questions is normally quite low, which is understandable as a student may feel uncomfortable being the centre of attention or judged by peers if they ask a 'silly' question. However, there will be times when you may need to ask questions related to aspects of a lecture you are unsure about. I often advise students to approach the lecturer afterwards or email them to enquire further if a question is too daunting; sometimes the opportunity just does not arise. The lecture format is sometimes not that effective at enhancing learning, as the opportunity for two-way communication and interactive learning is reduced.

Practical exams and viva voce

Many modules and programmes assess via practical exams or vivas. On our physiotherapy programme, there are practical exams where students may need to show assessment or treatment skills. We also have practical anatomy exams where students demonstrate their functional anatomy knowledge in demonstrating the actions of muscles or joints. I remember for my PhD viva that I had to answer questions and discuss concepts with three examiners, plus a chair of proceedings and my supervisor. The above assessment examples require public speaking skills, which are essential to communicate ideas and discuss concepts.

Many of the strategies in respect of knowing your subject, keeping it simple, and being enthusiastic and passionate would apply to practical exams and vivas. With these types of public speaking examples you will have no recourse to notes, audiovisuals or handouts, and therefore nowhere to hide or access material you should know when asked. The more authentic and comfortable you are with public speaking, the easier it will be for you to show your knowledge and expertise.

Employability and life skills

This type of public speaking activity is also very closely linked to job interviews. In an interview as in a viva or practical exam you will be asked questions and then expected to give appropriate answers. If you can answer confidently and show that you know and care about your subject, you should be in a better position to get the job. Employers may not just be seeking a correct reply, but also that you are authentic and can be trusted. It is not just what you say but also your public speaking approach that may be the key difference. Employers are also looking for people who would be good team players, and who may have other qualities apart from just knowledge and correct answers.

Extra-curricular activities

Apart from the above described university-based learning and teaching activities, you may be involved in extra-curricular activities. Examples include the student union chair or a committee member in a club or society, a student representative, peer-assisted learning leaders and student ambassador roles. Most of these roles will benefit from competent public speaking skills.

Student representative roles

In this role an elected student would represent fellow students from a cohort that may comprise large numbers of students. Student reps would often have to present and discuss issues with their cohort and represent student views to the respective university staff. Public speaking skills are essential here as without these it would be impossible to adequately represent your student colleagues across the university.

Peer-assisted learning (PAL) leaders

Many universities in the UK have students in Year 2 or beyond that support first-year students in their learning. These PAL leaders are often allocated to a group of students and assist in supporting them in covering and understanding material covered in their respective programmes. Standing up and presenting ideas and answering questions are all key public speaking skills for doing so.

Student ambassador roles

Our university and many in the UK interview and employ students in paid roles as student ambassadors. These roles require that students are comfortable speaking in public, from guided tours around a university campus to speaking to large groups of parents and respective students. Some students are on the same platform as senior university staff as part of the welcome team to audiences of well over a few hundred people.

Student Voice

Public speaking success

Example 1

'I have always been afraid of public speaking due to my speech impairment, so I have always avoided it. However, since doing the 'stand up and be heard' workshop and having learnt to be open about my speech impairment I have found it easier and more comfortable to speak in public both on a 1:1 or group basis.'

Example 2

'I thought I'd give you a little update. I did my first big presentation since your workshop last month at a conference in Canada; there were 45+ people in attendance and I was just fine. There are still areas for improvement, but I survived and didn't shake uncontrollably or stumble too much. Thank you again for all your advice.'

Overview of public speaking benefits

Hopefully this chapter will reinforce the message that although public speaking is a real fear for you, it is a key transferable skill that is necessary for your university career and future employment. One of my biggest motivations in writing this book was to encourage students to overcome or manage that fear of public speaking. It was ultimately to unlock that public speaking door that has been closed to many students and has prevented them from standing up and being heard.

Chapter summary

As an authentic public speaker, the benefits gained and uses for public speaking as discussed in this chapter will become more apparent and ensure a positive university experience. You will in turn be able to take this important life skill into most areas of employment and use it to enhance and not limit your career choices. Becoming an authentic public speaker is not an overnight process, but hopefully by following the previously discussed simple strategies in this study guide and altering your mindset it is clearly achievable. Many of our students on the SUBH workshops have benefitted from being an authentic public speaker and hopefully you will too (I certainly have!). Finally, please do not forget to complete the reflective space at the end of this chapter that focuses on the benefits of public speaking both for your university life and in the future.

Reflective Space

Using this reflective space will give you an opportunity to review and consolidate what has been covered in this chapter. This might be something that you have not done much of, but in in my experience and those of students in the SUBH workshops, it has proved really helpful.

What could you take home from this chapter in respect of the benefits of public speaking for your university life and beyond?

Appendix

Basics Chronological Checklist before, during and after your presentation (Chapter 5)

✓ *Tick each action/task* once it is completed. Most of the actions/tasks outlined below are basics that are often neglected. The **actions/tasks* are not basics, but are covered in more detail in other chapters; they are incorporated to show the whole picture.

Day(s) before the presentation

☐ Have you read the module assessment guidelines?

☐ *Have you practised your presentation (see Chapter 7)?

☐ Do you have a copy and backup of your presentation software (PowerPoint, Prezi, Slidebeam, Flowfella) on your USB or online (email, iCloud, etc.)?

☐ Have you checked that your presentation is easy to download onto a PC and is not faulty?

☐ Have you constructed your presentation slides effectively?

☐ Do you have a copy of your presentation slides or will you be using notes?

☐ Does the assessor/examiner require a copy of your PowerPoint/Prezi slides?

Night before and morning of the presentation

☐ Did you have a good night's sleep the night before?

☐ Did you set the alarm clock or phone to wake up in time?

☐ Did you have your clothes laid out the night before?

☐ Apart from wearing appropriate clothing for the occasion, is this comfortable?

☐ Hope you did not skip breakfast?

- ☐ Did you consider the traffic and how you will get to university on time?
- ☐ Presume you have checked and know which room on campus your presentation is in?
- ☐ Have you had a toilet break before your presentation or know where the nearest toilet facilities are?
- ☐ Presume you arrived at the venue a good 30+ minutes before?
- ☐ Have you ensured you uploaded your presentation onto the PC, projector and university IT system with enough time to spare?
- ☐ Have you asked the IT or academic staff if you are not sure where to upload your presentation?
- ☐ Presume you have checked that the presentation is correctly projected onto the screen?
- ☐ If you are using any online links to websites or resources, have you ensured the links are working before your presentation starts?

Presentation is about to start

- ☐ If using a pointer or remote slide control, have you plugged it in and does it work?
- ☐ Have you remembered your notes or prompt cards?
- ☐ Do you have a bottle of water or something to drink if needed?
- ☐ Have you taken enough breaths if you feel the nervousness about to start?
- ☐ Where and how are you standing in the room?
- ☐ *Have you taken on board the nonverbal information (Chapter 6) in this study guide?
- ☐ Any thoughts about the audience?
- ☐ How will you start your presentation?
- ☐ *Have you followed the strategies to be an authentic speaker (see Chapters 3 and 4)?
- ☐ *Are you still taking into account the nonverbal information and acting on it (Chapter 6)?

- ☐ Is there a clear structure to your presentation?
- ☐ Have you followed the timing guidelines and made sure you are sticking to your allocated time?
- ☐ Are you using your presentation slides effectively?
- ☐ Presume you are clear on how you will end your presentation?
- ☐ Are you prepared for questions and have you thought about how to answer them?

During the presentation

- ☐ *Have you followed the strategies to be an authentic speaker (see Chapters 3 and 4)?
- ☐ *Are you still taking into account the nonverbal information and acting on it (Chapter 6)?
- ☐ Is there a clear structure to your presentation?
- ☐ Have you followed the timing guidelines and made sure you are sticking to your allocated time?
- ☐ Are you using your presentation slides effectively?
- ☐ Presume you are clear on how you will end your presentation?
- ☐ Are you prepared for questions and have you thought about how to answer them?

After the presentation

- ☐ Did you reflect on your presentation?
- ☐ Did you read the feedback from your examiner/s and reflect on how it could have been improved?

Further Resources

Below is a list of online resources that may be useful to you in relation to your public speaking fear. Some of these resources or related activities have been discussed in this study guide.

Mindfulness Resources

Mindfulness has been briefly discussed in this study guide and below are a few resources you may find useful:

Headspace – popular mindfulness, free meditation app that many students may find helpful for stress and anxiety, www.headspace.com/

Mindfulness for students – this website is aimed at students and is full of resources, http://mindfulnessforstudents.co.uk/

For recommended books and CDs on mindfulness, http://mindfulnessforstudents.co.uk/resources/mindfulness-resources-for-students/

NHS NTW – this website has audio resources on a number of topics including mindfulness and visualisation, www.ntw.nhs.uk/pic/relax.php

Physical Activity/Exercise Resources

As covered in this study guide, exercise and being physically active/fit are important in preparing you for public speaking and in reducing your public speaking fear.

Get active for mental wellbeing – great exercise resource from the NHS, www.nhs.uk/conditions/stress-anxiety-depression/mental-benefits-of-exercise/

British active students survey report 2017/18 – please see the link below to access the full report that states the importance of physical activity for student mental wellbeing which is very relevant in decreasing and managing public speaking fear, www.precor.com/sites/default/files/BASS%20report%20FINALA.PDF

SAM App

An app developed by the University of the West of England (UWE) which may help you understand and manage anxiety, http://sam-app.org.uk/

TED and TEDx Talks

This is a fantastic resource with many video examples of public speaking, including some discussed in this study guide and referred to in the SUBH workshops. I would strongly advise you search for TED/TEDx Talks online and discover for yourself the great examples and lessons on public speaking.

Below, are a few examples of TED/TEDx Talks that I would recommend. Note that there are many more that you would find of use and that those in this list may be replaced in time by other suitable videos:

'The Power of Vulnerability', Brené Brown (TEDx Houston, 2010)

Vulnerability is a strength and requires courage, www.ted.com/talks/brene_brown_on_vulnerability

'The Science of Stage Fright and How to Overcome It', Michael Cho (TED-Ed, 2013)

Explains the physiology related to fear of public speaking, www.ted.com/talks/mikael_cho_the_science_of_stage_fright_and_how_to_overcome_it

'Your Body Language May Shape Who you Are', Amy Cuddy (TED Global, 2012)

Interesting ideas on how the body can influence the mind, www.ted.com/talks/amy_cuddy_your_body_language_shapes_who_you_are?referrer=playlist-before_public_speaking

'The Secret Structure of Great Talks', Nancy Duarte (TEDx East, 2011)

Discusses the value of ideas in a talk, www.ted.com/talks/nancy_duarte_the_secret_structure_of_great_talks?referrer=playlist-how_to_make_a_great_presentation#t-91871

'Grit: The Power of Passion and Perseverance', Angela Lee Duckworth (TED Talks Education, 2013)

Very relevant in respect of public speaking fear and not giving up, www.ted.com/talks/angela_lee_duckworth_grit_the_power_of_passion_and_perseverance

'The 7 Secrets of the Greatest Speakers in History', Richard Greene (TEDx Orange Coast, 2014)

Shares the secrets of public speaking, including public speaking is a conversation that we are passionate about, www.youtube.com/watch?v=i0a61wFaF8A

'How I Beat Stage Fright', Joe Kowan (TED@ State Street, 2013)

Humorous account on how to use music to conquer the fear of public speaking, www.ted.com/talks/joe_kowan_how_i_beat_stage_fright

'The 110 Techniques of Communication and Public Speaking', David J.P. Phillips (TEDx Zagreb, 2019)

Original presentation with some of the presenter`s favourite techniques, www.youtube.com/watch?v=K0pxo-dS9Hc

'How to Present to Keep your Audience's Attention', Mark Robinson (TEDx Eindhoven, 2016)

Use of questions in a presentation and storytelling, www.youtube.com/watch?v=BmEiZadVNWY

'How Public Speaking Will Change Your Life', Bridget Sampson (TEDx CSUN, 2017)

Inspiring presentation that avoids perfection in public speaking but shows the benefits of public speaking as a life skill, www.youtube.com/watch?v=ioTo11P0P9g

References

Adams, J. (2018) More college students seem to be majoring in perfectionism, *The New York Times, 18 January*, www.nytimes.com/2018/01/18/well/family/more-college-students-seem-to-be-majoring-in-perfectionism.html

American Psychiatric Association (2013) *Diagnostic and Statistical Manual of Mental Disorders* (5th edn). Arlington, VA: APA.

Ayres, J. and Ayres, D.M. (1994) The role of performance visualization in the basic public speaking course: current applications and future possibilities, *Basic Communication Course Annual*, *17*(6): 1–11.

Ayres, J. and Hopf, T.S. (1985) Visualization: A means of reducing speech anxiety. *Communication Education*, *34*: 318–23.

Ayres, J. and Hopf, T.S. (1989) Visualization: is it more than extra-attention? *Communication Education*, *38*(1): 1–5.

Ayres, J. and Ayres Sonandre, D.M. (2003) Performance visualization: does the nature of the speech model matter? *Communication Research Reports*, *20*(3): 260–8.

Bailey, E. (2019) A historical view of the pedagogy of public speaking, *Voice and Speech Review*, *13*(1): 31–42.

Branham, R.J. and Pearce, W.B. (1996) The conversational frame in public address, *Communication Quarterly*, *44*(4): 423–39.

Brown, B. (2015) *Daring Greatly: How the Courage to Be Vulnerable Transforms the Way We Live, Love, Parent, and Lead*. Harmondsworth: Penguin Random House.

Brown, K.W. and Ryan, R.M. (2003) The benefits of being present: mindfulness and its role in psychological well-being, *Journal of Personality and Social Psychology*, *84*(4): 822–48.

Chapman University (2018) The complete list of fears, 2018', Wilkinson Research Centre, www.chapman.edu/wilkinson/research-centers/babbie-center/_files/fear-2018/americas-top-fears-2018-ranked.pdf

Cocozza, P. (2018) 'My brain feels like it's been punched': the intolerable rise of perfectionism, *Guardian*, www.theguardian.com/society/2018/jul/17/my-brain-feels-like-its-been-punched-the-intolerable-rise-of-perfectionism

Consolo, K., Fusner, S. and Staib, S. (2008) Effects of diaphragmatic breathing on stress levels of nursing students, *Teaching and Learning in Nursing*, *3*(2): 67–71.

Cuddy, A.J.C., Wilmuth, C.A. and Carney, D.R. (2012) The benefit of power posing before a high-stakes social evaluation, Harvard Business School Working Paper.

Curran, T. and Hill, A.P. (2017) Perfectionism is increasing over time: a meta analysis of birth cohort differences from 1989 to 2016, *Psychological Bulletin*, *145*(4): 410–29.

Dwyer, K.K. and Davidson, M.M. (2012) Is public speaking really more feared than death?, *Communication Research Reports*, *29*(2): 99–107.

Ferreira Marinho, A.C., Mesquita de Medeiros, A., Côrtes Gama, A.C. and Caldas Teixeira, L. (2017) Fear of public speaking: perception of college students and correlates, *Journal of Voice*, *31*(1): e7–.e11.

Gallo, C. (2014) *Talk Like TED: The 9 Public-Speaking Secrets of the World's Top Minds*. London: St. Martin's Press.

Grieve, R. (2012) Stand up and be heard, International Stuttering Awareness Online Conference (ISAD12), 22 October, www.mnsu.edu/comdis/isad16/papers/grieve16.html

Grieve, R., Woodley, J., Hunt, S., McKay, A. and Lloyd, J. (2019) Student fear of public speaking in higher education: a qualitative survey, Advance HE Surveys Conference, Bristol, UK, 8 May.

Kernis, M.H. and Goldman, B.M. (2006) A multicomponent conceptualization of authenticity: theory and research, *Advances in Experimental Social Psychology*, *38*: 283–357.

Kushner, M. (2004) *Public Speaking for Dummies* (2nd edn). Hoboken, NJ: Wiley.

LeFebvre, L., LeFebvre, L.E. and Allen, M. (2018) Training the butterflies to fly in formation: cataloguing student fears about public speaking, *Communication Education*, *67*(3): 348–62.

Martin, N. (2003) *Essential Biological Psychology*. New York: Hodder Education/Oxford University Press.

Matsumoto, D. and Hwang, H.C. (2016) The cultural bases of nonverbal communication, in D. Matsumoto, H.C. Hwang and M.G. Frank (eds), *APA Handbooks in Psychology: APA Handbook of Nonverbal Communication*. Washington, DC: American Psychological Association.

McNeill, D. (2008) *Gesture and Thought* (3rd edn). Chicago: University of Chicago Press.

Mengers, A.A. (2014) The benefits of being yourself: an examination of authenticity, uniqueness, and well-being, in *Master of Applied Positive Psychology (MAPP), Capstone Projects*: 63.

Motley, M.T. and Molloy, J.L.T. (1994) An efficacy test of a new therapy ('communication-orientation motivation') for public speaking anxiety, *Journal of Applied Communication Research*, *22*(1): 48–58.

Ni, P. (2013) 5 tips to reduce the fear of public speaking, *Psychology Today*, www.psychologytoday.com/gb/blog/communication-success/201311/5-tips-reduce-the-fear-public-speaking

Pearson, J.E. (2007) Reframing three major fears about public speaking, *Toastmaster*, December: 25–27.

Plasencia, M.L., Taylor, C.T. and Alden, L.E. (2016) Unmasking one's true self facilitates positive relational outcomes: authenticity promotes social approach processes in Social Anxiety Disorder, *Clinical Psychological Science*, *4*(6): 1002–14.

Race, P. (2015) *The Lecturer's Toolkit: A Practical Guide to Assessment, Learning and Teaching* (4th edn). Abingdon: Routledge.

Rattine-Flaherty, E. (2014) Participatory sketching as a tool to address students' public speaking anxiety, *Communication Teacher*, *28*(1): 26–31.

Russell, G. and Topham, P. (2012) The impact of social anxiety on student learning and well-being in higher education, *Journal of Mental Health*, *21*(4): 375–85.

Souter, K. (2011) *How You Can Talk to Anyone: Teach Yourself*. London: Hodder Education.

Taylor, E. (2000) *Encyclopaedia of Psychology*, Vol. 2. Washington, DC: Oxford University Press.

Watson, P. (1973) What people usually fear, *The Sunday Times*.

Willis, J. and Todorov, A. (2006) Making up your mind after a 100Ms exposure to a face, *Psychological Science*, *17*(7): 592–98.

Index